# Getting to Know Buddhism

# GETTING TO KNOW BUDDHISM

*by*

## Sunthorn Plamintr, PhD

**BUDDHADHAMMA FOUNDATION**
**BANGKOK THAILAND**

**Buddhadhamma Foundation**
© **By Sunthorn Plamintr, PhD**
Published in 1994.
Printed in Thailand


ISBN      974 - 89086 - 3 - 1


*First impression*                                    *August, 1994*
*Second impression*                               *April, 1996*
*Third impression*                                 *October, 1997*
*Fourth Impression*                              *October, 1998*


**Published by:**
**Buddhadhamma Foundation,**
87/126 Tesabahl Songkroh Rd., Lad Yao, Chatuchak, BANGKOK, 10900, THAILAND
Tel. : (66–2) 589–9012, 580–2719; Fax : (66–2) 954-4791
**Printed at:**
**Sahadhammika Ltd.,**
54/8-9 Jaran Sanitwong 12, Jaran Sanitwong Rd, Tha Phra, Bangkok Yai, Bangkok.
Tel. (66-2) 412-3087


Photographs on pages 1, 2, 22, 40, 84, 132, 156, and 184 courtesy of Wat Sanghatahn,
Nonthaburi, Thailand

# Contents

# The Dhamma     63

# The Saṅgha     85

# Kamma 109

# The Five Precepts   133

# Meditation   157

# Buddhism and Thai society      185

# PREFACE

The present volume is intended, as the name implies, to benefit newcomers to Buddhism who wish to gain an introduction to the religion and its practice. I have tried to present the various subjects from the perspective of the Pali canonical literature and related commentaries of the Theravada tradition, which is generally regarded the more orthodox form of Buddhism prevalent in Thailand, Sri Lanka, Burma, Laos and Cambodia.

I have also made occasional use of the following in preparing the manuscript for the present work: Venerable Phra Dhammapiṭaka (Prayudh Payutto)'s *Thai Buddhism in the Buddhist World* and A *Dictionary of Buddhism;* Venerable Gunaratane's *Mindfulness in Plain English;* and Professor G.P. Mallalasekara's *Dictionary of Pali Proper Names.* To all of them I wish to express my profound indebtedness. Thanks and appreciation are also due to Mr. Bruce Evans, who has kindly offered many valuable suggestions and painstakingly edited the work to make it more presentable to the reading public and, last but not least, to the Buddhadhamma Foundation, which has made it possible for the book to see the light of day.

May all beings be happy. May the Buddha's words spread far and wide for the benefit of all mankind.

Sunthorn Plamintr, PhD.

# 1

# INTRODUCTION

## BUDDHISM: SOME SALIENT FEATURES

RELIGIONS, IT IS OFTEN OBSERVED, ARE products of fear. This fear is in turn based on ignorance. With the dawn of wisdom and the ever-expanding horizons of knowledge, faith and confidence in religions begin to evaporate, like morning mist under the rising sun. As William Macquitty puts it, "With the advance of science and psychology many of the older faiths have suffered. Their beliefs went against the new knowledge and the new knowledge won."

Not so with Buddhism. Buddhism is a result of the human quest for the ultimate truth, an aspiration for that which is the highest and noblest in life. It is based on the Buddha's wisdom, on his enlightenment, attained through the complete eradication of ignorance, fear and all other defilements from his mind. His teachings, called the Dhamma (Sanskrit: Dharma), have stood the test of time for more than twenty-five centuries. It is with deep faith and conviction in the Buddha's teachings that Francis Story, a British scholar, asserts:

"The doctrines of Buddha Dhamma stand today, as unaffected by the march of time and the expansion of knowledge as when they were first enunciated. No matter to what lengths increased scientific knowledge can extend man's mental horizon, within the framework of the Dhamma there is room for the acceptance and assimilation of further discovery."

One of the most outstanding features of Buddhism is its total independence of divine elements. It is a religion of self-help. According to Buddhism, human beings should learn to be self-reliant and to have faith in their own ability. Buddhist philosophy is anthropocentric in its outlook and practical implementation, placing man at the centre of its metaphysical and ethical systems. It is a religion that insists primarily on man's own effort and perseverance to achieve his goals, be they material or spiritual, rather than prayer or wishful thinking.

As Venerable Dr. H. Gunaratana points out, "Buddhism as a whole is quite different from the theological religions with which Westerners are most familiar. It is a direct entrance to a spiritual or divine realm without addressing deities or other 'agents.' Its flavor is intensely clinical, much more akin to what we would call psychology than to what we would usually call religion. It is an ever-ongoing investigation of reality, a microscopic examination of the very process of perception. Its intention is to pick apart the screen of lies and delusions through which we normally view the world, and thus to reveal the face of ultimate reality."

Those who have studied Buddhism often claim, with some justification, that Buddhism is scientific in nature. It is certainly the most scientific of all religions. Its teachings are logical and its methods are compatible with scientific methods. That is why many modern scientists and thinkers believe that the teachings of the Buddha are still valid and practical in spite of their great age. The Dhamma is an ancient spiritual legacy that can benefit mankind as much today as it did more than twenty-five centuries ago.

Blind faith is abhorrent to Buddhism, which clearly urges us to think freely and not to accept things blindly. In Buddhism, free thought is upheld, questions are welcome, and positive doubt is considered the first stepping stone to wisdom. Buddhism believes in human potential. It also asserts human equality, emphasizing personal and social responsibilities, based on the doctrine of *kamma* (Sanskrit: *karma*—action and result).

Kindness, compassion, and tolerance are some of the virtues that Buddhism strongly encourages. This explains why Buddhists are generally peace-loving people and why religious war is unknown in the long history of Buddhism. Much of the suffering in the world today is a direct result of the lack of these qualities. Religions that should be serving to unite people and maintain harmony are instead being used to divide and alienate them from each other. The history of some religions is full of bloodshed and violence. Against this unfortunate background, Buddhism stands out as the most tolerant religion in the annals of human civilization. "Alone of all the great world religions," observes Aldous Huxley, "Buddhism made its way without persecution, censorship or inquisition."

## THE BUDDHIST ATTITUDE

In Buddhism, right attitude is closely connected with understanding and knowledge. It is founded on wisdom. With right attitude we see Buddhism not simply as a system of beliefs, but a teaching that offers an effective system for exploring reality and the deeper levels of mind, one that leads to the very foundation of consciousness itself. This naturally entails an element of penetrative insight and constant awareness. In addition to these more profound teachings, Buddhism also presents us with a system of rituals which are the natural result of over twenty-five centuries of cultural growth and development.

Because Buddhism is a religion of self-help, the first and foremost duty of a Buddhist is to understand the supreme position of the human being and one's responsibility toward both oneself and fellow sentient beings. The Buddha did not claim any divine affinity. His enlightenment was a result of his own efforts, unaided by teachers or divine providence. There was no need for him to base his teachings on divine revelation, as is usually done by religious teachers and prophets. The Dhamma that he expounded is the Truth itself—to introduce divine elements into it would be a superfluous exercise. His realization of the Dhamma and the validity of the teaching itself are the strength of his teachings, and this has rendered so-called divine inspiration or intervention irrelevant in the Buddhist context.

According to Buddhism, humanity's position is supreme. Human beings are their own masters, endowed with great potential, from mundane material concerns up to the highest spiritual achievements. This position is clearly exemplified by the Buddha's own struggles and successes. He attributed his enlightenment and all his achievements to human effort, not to divine grace. It is encouraging to know that, according to the Buddha, only a human being can become a Buddha, a position to which even gods and deities cannot aspire. Every human being possesses the seed of Buddha-nature, the potential to become a Buddha, and that potential can only be actualized through human endeavor.

The Buddha's assertion, unique and unparalleled in the history of religions, presupposes the principle of individual responsibility. Because man is supreme, a master of his own destiny, it follows that he must also be responsible for his own action and inaction. "You must walk the path yourself," says the Buddha, "the *Tathāgata* (Buddha) only points the way."

Sometimes this statement is misconstrued to imply the Buddha's inability, or unwillingness, to be of real assistance to his followers. It is pointed out that in contrast with other religious teachers, prophets, or even deities, whose alleged role is that of a 'saviour,' the function of the Buddha is merely that of a teacher, giving instruction and little else. This criticism is based on ignorance of the real personality and spiritual power of the Buddha on the one hand, and blind faith in the so-called saviour on the other. Even in so simple a matter as quenching thirst or hunger, one has to consume drinks or food oneself: is it not curious that one would look to an outside saviour to fulfill one's larger and more profound needs? The problem becomes more complex when the saviour has to respond to millions of prayers all at once, many of which are locked in conflicting interests. The Buddha was too honest and straightforward to suggest that anyone other than oneself, even a God (if one does exist), could be of real assistance if one fails to take responsibility for one's own actions. "You are your own refuge, who else could be your refuge?" These are the Buddha's words, as true and valid today as when they were pronounced by the Master more than 2,500 years ago.

Right attitude is possible only in a framework of freedom of thought, another prominent feature of Buddhist philosophy, and freedom of thought is possible only in the context of trust and confidence. The extent that freedom of thought is encouraged by the Buddha is uniquely characteristic of both the religion and its founder: not only did he insist that his disciples examine and reexamine his teachings, but he was willing even to subject himself and his character to their close scrutiny. Only a teacher of the highest impeccability could allow such an investigation.

Freedom of thought should therefore be considered an integral ingredient of the Buddhist attitude. This quality is essential in the context of Buddhism, which is known for its scientific approach. Like a good scientist, a Buddhist should constantly examine the Dhamma and experiment with its principles through practical application, by rationalizing and investigating them with an open mind. It is through such a process that faith and conviction, based on wisdom, will grow and become strengthened. To blindly believe, without exercising one's own reasoning faculties and without attempting at a direct experience, is, according to Buddhism, counterproductive to the development of wisdom.

Since freedom of thought occupies an important place in the Buddhist system, this naturally leads to another essential characteristic of the religion. A religious attitude rooted in freedom of thought points to religious tolerance, or tolerance with regard to the views and opinions of others. This explains why Buddhists are usually very tolerant people and why their religion has spread peacefully through the ages.

The Dhamma is like a raft, says the Buddha. It is used for crossing the river of pain, suffering, and conflict. Once the crossing has been accomplished, it is not necessary to cling onto the raft or carry it around. With such broad minded attitudes and intellectual maturity, Buddhists can share room on the 'raft' of Dhamma with others, without stubbornly holding on to it and arguing with one another as to the quality and the beauty of different 'rafts.'

Buddhism views all phenomena in terms of causal relationship. This means that all phenomena, all occurrences, whether empirically perceivable or otherwise, are subject to the law of cause and effect. Everything is conditioned by causal factors, and all things are themselves conditioning factors for other occurrences. Nothing is absolutely independent, for, according to the Buddhist philosophy, absolute existence is not possible.

Based on this principle of causal relationship, it naturally follows that all phenomena are interrelated and interdependent. One single event, trifling and insignificant as it may seem, may in fact be related to thousands of other events, and this relationship may extend, in the final analysis, to all other conceivable phenomena, even though they may seem as remote as the wildest imagination can stretch. Thus, Buddhism perceives all lives, human as well as nonhuman, and all things and events, not as independent entities, but rather as part and parcel of the whole cosmic order, interconnected in an infinitely complex relationship by the common law of conditionality.

Buddhist attitude allows for the growth of mutual understanding, trust and a deep sense of altruistic consideration. Selfishness and greed are the usual negative ramifications of a narrow world view, based on the philosophy of narcissistic hedonism. Buddhist philosophy is an antidote to this. It poses universal compassion as the foundation and driving motivation for social responsibility and action.

Buddhists regard the Buddha as the greatest teacher, the Dhamma, his great teachings, and the Saṅgha, his well-trained followers. The Buddha has shown the way, having himself gone before, but it is up to us to walk that way ourselves. This is a responsibility that each and every person must undertake individually. A Buddhist should maintain a scientific attitude, questioning, investigating, and experimenting with the Dhamma to develop full understanding of the Buddha's teachings. Practice of the Dhamma should be properly grounded on wisdom and supported by a conviction that all that is noble and good can be achieved by one's own efforts. Even the highest level of spiritual attainment, Buddhahood, is not beyond reach of those who persevere in their efforts.

## OBJECTS OF WORSHIP

There is a Pali term *tiratana,* which means 'three gems' or 'three treasures.' This word *tiratana* is used to designate the three objects of highest respect in the Buddhist religion: they are the Buddha, the Dhamma, and the Saṅgha. Usually, they are collectively referred to in English as the Triple Gem. Buddhists in all traditions regard the Triple Gem with great devotion and respect.

Buddha means the Enlightened One. He is the embodiment of virtues and goodness and the founder of the religion of Buddhism. Endowed with the three qualities of infinite wisdom, perfect purity, and universal compassion, he bequeathed to mankind a teaching that is unequalled in history. This is the Dhamma, the Universal Law of Truth, which the Buddha had discovered and which forms the basis of the Buddhist way of life and spiritual practice. The Saṅgha is the community of those noble disciples, the Holy Order, who have realized the Truth after the Buddha and who have attained a high degree of spiritual discipline.

The Buddha, the Dhamma, and the Saṅgha are our true refuges. They are so closely related that from the practical perspective they essentially form a unified principle rather than three separate entities. The arising of a Buddha is dependent upon the realization of the Dhamma, which is both an absolute condition and the essence of Buddhahood. The Buddha in the ultimate sense is therefore none other than the Dhamma itself. However, without a Buddha, the Dhamma would remain undiscovered and untaught; it would remain an abstract quality without any practical value as far as human beings are concerned.

It is through a Buddha that the Dhamma is made manifest and its existence becomes meaningful, just as the fragrance of a flower becomes manifest when there is someone to smell it. When the Buddha realized the Truth, the Dhamma acquired a meaningful character; when he expounded it, the Dhamma came to life and transformed into practical teachings. Thus the teachings of the Buddha are the Dhamma in its truest expression, which is intelligible, concrete, and practical.

The Saṅgha in turn depends on the Buddha and the Dhamma for its arising and existence. Members of the Saṅgha are 'born' through the realization of the Dhamma, following the Buddha's example. Thus the Saṅgha stands as the most crucial testimony to Buddhahood. Without the Saṅgha, Buddhahood would lack concrete and objective evidence in the eyes of the world and would therefore fall short of any practical purpose. As realization of the Truth constitutes being the Saṅgha, it therefore follows that without the Saṅgha, both Buddhahood and the Dhamma, which in the ultimate sense are one and the same, would lose much of their meaning and value. It is the Saṅgha that preserves and spreads the Dhamma. Since the Dhamma is the essence of Buddhism as revealed by the Buddha, and the Saṅgha provides it with a definite form, it is not difficult to see that without the Saṅgha the religion would not have been established in the first place, or if it were founded, it would not have continued for long after the historical Buddha was gone.

Buddhists regard the Triple Gem with the highest veneration. We pay respect to the Triple Gem by practising the Dhamma and conducting ourselves in accordance with the Buddha's teachings. We also support the Saṅgha so that the Dhamma will be further preserved and promoted for the welfare and benefit of the world.

## BUDDHIST PRACTICE AND GOAL

Buddhists believe in the cycle of birth and death, called *Saṁsāra* in Pali. This belief is based on the recognition of the continuity of a series of lives from the past to the present and from the present to the future. The present life is not the only one, and it does not dissolve into nothingness at death. *Saṁsāra* means that there existed lives prior to this one, and other existences will continue after this one's termination. The process and the continuity of life are sustained by the force of *kamma*, wilful action based on desire, attachment and ignorance. This instinctive clinging to life, which is a universal attribute, is a determining factor for the continuation of existence.

*Saṁsāra* also implies a plurality of different realms of existence, in which rebirth takes place according to the nature of kammic energy. Some planes of existence are painful, and are a result of evil and unwholesome *kamma*, while others are filled with happiness and pleasurable experiences, and are attained through the positive energy of wholesome *kamma*. The human realm is one which

11

contains a mixture of experiences, both pleasurable and painful, and this realm is shared by animals of different kinds.

*Saṁsāra* can be also interpreted to refer to the changing states of consciousness within the mind. Some scholars construe *Saṁsāra* to signify the stream of experiences that come within the sphere of perception. Thus, according to these interpretations, *Saṁsāra* may either be viewed simply as a state of consciousness, or the many experiences with which an individual becomes involved. It follows then that there may be many births and deaths occurring from moment to moment in different planes of thought or experience.

The ultimate goal in Buddhist practice is to be free from this cycle of birth and death. *Saṁsāra* is considered undesirable as it lacks security and is liable to the vicissitudes and uncertainties of existence, such as old age, disease, death, pain, and suffering. Freedom from *Saṁsāra* is called *Nibbāna* (Sanskrit: *nirvana*), metaphorically described as the other shore, or the transcendental state beyond the confusion of worldly existence. It is the state which is completely free from conditionalities and limitations and is therefore not subject to all the conditions in mundane existence. *Nibbāna* is a transcendent state, unconditioned and absolute.

The cycle of birth and death is perpetuated by the force of *kamma*-producing defilements (*kilesa*), chiefly by ignorance, craving and attachment. To achieve *Nibbāna*, these defilements must be eliminated from the mind. This is by no means an easy task. The Buddha himself, even after his enlightenment, hesitated over teaching the Dhamma for some time, for he knew how his teachings went against the current of deluded thinking. He later said, "Few are those who have gone to the other shore, the rest are running up and down on this side." Thus, despite all the lofty ideals and exaltation of *Nibbāna*, not all Buddhists feel inclined to strive for it in this life. Many are content to follow some basic ethical principles, such as generosity and moral precepts, to accumulate positive *kamma* in the hope of being reborn in a happy realm of existence.

The Buddha mentions three desirable existential attainments (*sampatti*):

1. The attainment of a human state of existence (*manussa-sampatti*): The Buddha praised this kind of attainment as having the highest potential for spiritual growth and development.

2. The attainment of heavenly existence as a god or goddess (*deva-sampatti*): Although the heavenly planes of existence are endowed with all manner of pleasurable experiences and are relatively unaffected by sorrow and pain, as far as spiritual development is concerned this proves to be a disadvantage. Heavenly beings are likely to become intoxicated with the sensual pleasures constantly at their disposal. In such an atmosphere, training in spiritual practice is simply an improbable aspiration.

3. Attainment of *Nibbāna* (*Nibbāna-sampatti*): This is the noblest and most exalted of all attainments and is the ultimate goal in Buddhism.

Both human and heavenly realms are still within the sphere of mundane existence and are therefore subject to impermanence, change, and unsatisfactoriness. *Nibbāna* is transcendent and free from the attributes that characterize mundane states.

To achieve any of these attainments, it is necessary to follow the threefold training of morality (*sīla*), concentration (*samādhi*), and wisdom (*paññā*).

Buddhist morality refers to training in ethical conduct, entailing conscious restraint of bodily and verbal actions so that they cause harm neither to oneself nor to others. This is a fundamental level of training in Buddhism, especially for those who have dedicated themselves to a religious life. For laity the Buddha often recommended beginning the practice with generosity (*dāna*) as a means of acquiring a proper mental foundation for higher ethical discipline.

The main objectives of morality, according to Buddhism, are self-restraint, purity in personal conduct, and benevolent social interaction. Man is intrinsically wholesome, being of a noble-minded nature. The practice in Buddhist morality aims at preserving that natural state of humanity and wholesomeness. This is accomplished through the observance of certain sets of precepts that are graded into different levels according to different stages of moral maturity. Basically, lay Buddhists follow five precepts: not to kill, not to steal, to refrain from sexual misconduct, not to resort to falsehood, and to refrain from taking intoxicants. The essence of these precepts is moral responsibility to oneself and other beings.

Concentration or *samādhi* refers to mental discipline. This is a higher training than morality and generosity, as it deals directly with the mind and the deeper levels of consciousness. It entails control and mastery of the mind, which requires more intensive application of effort. Not many people nowadays are interested enough to commit themselves to the serious practice of concentration, although in recent times more and more have come to realize its benefits and have started to take part in the training.

Training in concentration involves one form of meditative discipline, while the development of wisdom concerns another. The Pali term for wisdom is *paññā*. It is the penetrative insight into reality, understanding things as they really are. This is the understanding of the Four Noble Truths, which is the highest wisdom, and which encompasses Truth in its totality. It is a higher knowledge, one which eliminates mental impurities at their very roots.

Metaphorically, defilements are compared to weeds, which are harmful to flowering plants. If the weeds overgrow them, the flowers will be suffocated. Practising morality (*sīla*) is comparable to keeping the weeds trimmed down and under control. Training in concentration (*samādhi*) is like keeping the weeds under a big rock, so that they have no chance to grow further. However, if one neglects trimming, or if the rock is removed, the weeds will grow back to their former verdant abundance. The development of wisdom (*paññā*) is like rooting out the weeds of defilements, chopping them up, and burning them to ashes so that they have no chance to bother the beautiful plant of the mind again.

According to Buddhism, *Nibbāna* is the highest goal of the religious life, the most complete security and the ultimate bliss. The Buddha defines this state of summum bonum as "the extinction of desire, the extinction of hatred, and the extinction of delusion." Individual worldlings wandering through *Saṁsāra* may have other objectives or aspirations in life, and may even perceive *Nibbāna* as irrelevant, but ultimately the journey will culminate in *Nibbāna*, even though it may take countless births and deaths and an unimaginable length of time. The Buddha referred to *Nibbāna* as "the complete destruction of that very 'thirst' (*taṇhā*), giving it up, renouncing it, being free from it, detaching from it," and as "the calming of all conditioned things, giving up of all defilements, cessation of craving, and detachment."

## A GLIMPSE AT EARLY BUDDHISM

Buddhism evolved and developed around the teachings of the Buddha. During his lifetime, the religion prospered and spread rapidly through the great personality of the founder himself, and he was assisted by a large and fast-growing community of noble disciples who drew inspiration from his example of renunciation and self-sacrifice. Before the Buddha passed away, the religion had become well established in India, the land of its birth, and the Master had the satisfaction of realizing that his teachings would continue to benefit the world after he was gone. After his death, his disciples took upon themselves the responsibility of carrying his message of love and wisdom to even farther corners of the earth. Through the centuries that followed, Buddhism emerged as the largest world religion and one of the most important civilizing forces in the history of mankind.

Originally, the Buddha's teachings were preserved and handed

15

down through oral tradition from one generation of monks to another, until they were committed into writing in Sri Lanka some five hundred years after the Great Demise. Councils were held from time to time, attended by large numbers of eminent and learned monks, to verify and confirm those teachings in order that their purity be preserved. Earlier councils were held in India, but as Buddhism spread to other countries and flourished, monks in those lands also took the initiative to keep up the tradition. The shift from oral tradition to literary format, which took place for the first time in Sri Lanka, made it possible for monks, as guardians of the religion, to ensure the authenticity of the Buddha's teachings through the subsequent centuries of its troubled history.

The fourth century BC saw India being invaded by a Western power. Alexander the Great (356-323 BC), having conquered part of the subcontinent, established Greek control in the country where Buddhism was flourishing and widespread. The Greek rule, however, was short lived. Chandragupta of the Mauryan dynasty vanquished the Greek power in India and largely expanded the Magadha empire. He was the grandfather of the mighty Emperor Ashoka, who ascended the Magadha throne in the year 218 after the passing away of the Buddha and ruled over the vast empire for forty-one years.

Ashoka was not born a Buddhist. He had been a ruthless King, known for his cruelty, whose insatiable ambition was to conquer more and more territories and expand his powers. His empire extended northeastward as far as Kamarupa (Assam), and included Kashmir as well as Nepal. On the northwest it stretched to include the lands of Paropanisadae (Kabul), Arachosia (Kandahar), Aria (Herat), and parts of Gedrosia (Baluchistan). In the south it covered almost the whole peninsular, down to the Penner river.

After his conversion to Buddhism, Ashoka became a changed man. He renounced the policy of Conquest by War (*yuddhavijaya*), which necessarily involved killing and destruction, and embarked upon the policy of Conquest by Dhamma (*dhammavijaya*), which subsequently became his lifelong passion and mission. Under his patronage, Buddhism prospered as never before. His stone inscriptions eloquently speak of the religious activities during his time, both within his empire as well as in other countries, with which he maintained a close diplomatic relationship. Thus, we have clear evidence today of the 'mission of piety' that he sent to many foreign lands, including five Greek countries, whose kings have been identified as Magas of Cyrene (300-258 BC), Ptolemy II of Egypt (285-247 BC), Antigonas Gonatas of Macedonia (276-246 BC), Alexander of Epirus (272-258 BC), and Antiochus II of Syria (261-246 BC).

It was under the auspices of Ashoka that the third Buddhist Council was held, presided over by his spiritual master, Venerable Moggalliputta Tissa, and attended by one thousand *Arahants* (enlightened beings). After the successful conclusion of the council, nine missions of elders were despatched to spread the Dhamma in various states and foreign countries. It was the first recorded instance of state-sponsored missionary activities in the history of religions. One of the missions, led by Venerables Sona and Uttara, arrived in Suvaṇṇabhumi, a country to the east of India. The administrative centre of Suvaṇṇabhumi has been identified as the province of Nakhon Pathom in central Thailand. The establishment of the religion there thus dates back as far as some twenty-three centuries ago.

## THE EMERGENCE OF MAHAYANA AND THERAVADA

With the passage of time there arose certain developments within the Buddhist Order that finally led to the formation of different sects. The Mahasanghikas came into existence toward the end of the first century after the Buddha's death. The other major school, which claimed to be orthodox and conservative, became known as Theravada. The school of the Mahasanghikas was later called

17

Mahayana. Out of these two sects, eighteen schools had evolved by the time Ashoka was crowned emperor of Magadha. Most of these were short-lived, and finally only the two schools Theravada and Mahayana survived and prospered, although they were again divided into numerous sub-sects in later times. It was the latter that was in due course introduced into Tibet, acquiring its own distinct flavor and characteristics as the Vajrayana school.

Questions are often asked as to differences between the two major traditions. To be sure, most of the differences are rather superficial, and can be observed in the way monks put on their monastic garments, the way ceremonies are conducted, the languages used to record the Buddha's teachings (Theravada adheres to the original Pali, while Mahayana uses Sanskrit), and all those cultural elements that have come to be associated with each denomination. On a deeper level, there are differences in the emphasis being placed on certain aspects of the Buddha's teachings and in the methods of religious training. Thus, while Theravada stresses the importance of monastic discipline as the preliminary requisite for higher spiritual development, Mahayana saw the need to modify and adapt it in accordance with the changing circumstances. The Bodhisattva ideals, though accepted and taught in the Theravada tradition, are much more strongly emphasized in the Mahayana system and are considered central to their religious practice.

But generally speaking, both Theravada and Mahayana traditions have more things in common than meets the eye, especially from the doctrinal perspective. Both agree on the teachings which are fundamental in the Buddhist system, such as the four Noble Truths, the Noble Eightfold Path, the ten Perfections (six in Mahayana), the four Foundations of Mindfulness, the twelve links of Dependent Origination, the Law of Conditionality, the nature of enlightenment, *Nibbāna* as the summum bonum of religious training, the doctrines of *kamma* and rebirth, etc. Both accept the roles of compassion and wisdom as crucial in any aspiration to enlightenment. Both uphold the cultivation of such virtues as kindness, gratitude, respect to elders, humility, altruism, generosity, morality, mindfulness, non-attachment, universal compassion, and so forth. It is therefore proper to conclude that all the different schools of Buddhism uniformly correspond with one another in essential doctrines, objectives, practice, and goals.

Theravada Buddhism flourished in southern countries such as Sri Lanka, Myanmar (Burma), Thailand, Laos, and Cambodia, while the Mahayana school spread northward to Nepal, China, Tibet, Mongolia, Korea, Japan and Vietnam. The former is thus sometimes referred to as the Southern School, and the latter as the Northern School. Tibet's Vajrayana is currently so widespread in the West that it has come to be recognized in its own right as a separate denomination, distinct from Mahayana to which it was earlier closely affiliated.

## BUDDHISM IN THAILAND

Buddhism was introduced into Thailand some twenty-three centuries ago when the region was still populated by Mons and Lawas. Nakhon Pathom was then the administrative centre and, after the advent of the religion, became an active seat of Buddhist propagation. Later the region was occupied by the Thais, also followers of Buddhism; Khun Luang Mao, who ruled over the Ailao Kingdom about two thousand years ago, was the first Thai Buddhist king and the professed upholder of the religion.

Mahayana Buddhism spread to Thailand in the 9th century during the reign of the Srivijaya kings, who ruled from Sumatra and whose territories extended over some southern provinces of Thailand. Meanwhile the Khmer authority and influence also spread over the whole of central and northeastern Thailand. The Khmer kings were adherents of Mahayana Buddhism, which had by then absorbed much of the Brahmanistic elements into its

19

system. It was around this time that Mahayana Buddhism and Brahmanism began to exert deep influence on the Thai culture. Although neither of them came to replace Theravada Buddhism, their cultural influences were considerable, and can be readily observed even today.

Another stream of cultural and religious influences began to flow into Thailand from Myanmar (Burma) around the 11th century when King Anuruddha ascended the Myanmar throne. His territorial conquests stretched as far as the Thai kingdoms of Lanna and Lanchang. Another form of Theravada Buddhism, called Pukam or Pagan Buddhism, which was practised by the Myanmar people, spread into these lands. Following the decline of the Khmer and Myanmar influences, there emerged in the 13th century the kingdoms of Lanna in the north and Sukhothai in north-central Thailand. At the height of its glory Lanna became an important seat of Buddhist learning, where numerous scholarly works in Pali were produced. The most famous king of Sukhothai was Ramkamhaeng the Great, who unified the Thai people under one single rule and whose territories extended far and wide. He strongly supported the form of Theravada Buddhism prevalent in Sri Lanka, which by then had spread to Thailand following a general reform under the auspices of King Parakramabahu the Great. Lanka Buddhism, as it was called, became highly popular in Thailand and virtually replaced other forms of Buddhism in the country. This is the form of Buddhism preserved and practised in the present time. Later, during the Ayutthaya period, when religious conditions in Sri Lanka deteriorated so much that not a single monk could be found on the island, Thailand had the opportunity to more than repay this spiritual debt. A delegation of monks, headed by Venerable Upāli, was despatched to Sri Lanka to help revive the monastic order in that country. The ecclesiastical lineage so reestablished became known as the Siam Sect, the country's largest denomination today.

Thus the history of Thai Buddhism may be divided into four

periods. The first was Theravada Buddhism as introduced by Ashoka's mission; the second was Mahayana Buddhism under the Srivijaya and Khmer influences; the third was Pukam Buddhism introduced from Myanmar, and the fourth, Theravada Buddhism from Sri Lanka.

# 2

# GENERAL OUTLINE

## HISTORICAL PERSPECTIVE OF BUDDHISM

THE WORD BUDDHISM IS DERIVED FROM *Buddha*, meaning the Enlightened One or the Awakened One. Buddha is not a proper name, but a generic term or appellative, referring to a founder of a religion, one who has attained supreme enlightenment and who is regarded as superior to all other beings, human or divine, by virtue of his knowledge of the Truth (Dhamma). Buddhism is therefore not just a faith, but a religion based on supreme enlightenment; it is a system of teachings and practice with enlightenment as its ultimate goal.

From its origins in India, Buddhism spread far and wide to various parts of the world. At one time it was the largest world religion, commanding one fifth of the total world population. As such it was one of the greatest civilizing forces the world has known. As H.G. Wells puts it, "Buddhism has done more for the advance of world civilization than any other influence in the chronicles of mankind." Today, it has become increasingly popular in the United States and other countries in the West. Its current following is reported to be over 300 millions.

Buddhism arose within the cultural milieus of Brahmanism, which came to be known in its present form as Hinduism. But Buddhism was a separate religion, never an offshoot of the older faith, as sometimes claimed by historians. Buddhism deeply influenced Hinduism, which later incorporated much of the Buddhist thought into its own philosophical system, and succeeded, through centuries of relentless persecution and assimilation, in replacing Buddhism as India's major religion. It is also believed by some Christian scholars that Buddhism may have exerted an influence on early Christianity, when it spread westward from India during the reign of Ashoka, some two centuries before the birth of Jesus Christ, and flourished in the regions where Christ grew up, till the early days of Christianity. There is a strong belief among some scholars that in his early years Christ may have even studied and trained under Buddhist masters of the time. There are, of course, many who refute this idea.

## INSTITUTIONAL MAKEUP

An institutional religion is normally characterized by certain elements that go to make up the whole. Generally, these include the founder, the teachings, the congregation of followers, the system of worship (including rites and ceremonies), the religious sanctuaries, and the sacred objects within the framework of that particular religion. The Buddhist institution, with its own distinct character and culture, fits this description, being a complete system of thought and training.

The Buddha was the founder of Buddhism. Some religions, such as Hinduism, cannot ascribe their establishment to any one personality, owing their existence to an ancient tradition, the origin of which has long been lost in antiquity. Of those which are founded on a historical personality, their founders mostly claim affinity to, and connection with, a divine power, and are therefore compelled to demand unquestioning faith from their followers. The Buddha was a historical personality who made no such claims and who taught his followers without subscribing to any divine grace or supernatural powers.

The Buddha's teachings are known as the Dhamma. In fact, this is the most important ingredient in the Buddhist religious system. As Buddhism is a religion based on knowledge and enlightenment, the validity and value of the Dhamma naturally assume prime significance in the whole system as opposed to belief and faith, as in theistic religions.

The followers or believers form another important component of a religion, for without them the religion would prove of little benefit. In Buddhism, the congregation is broadly divided into two groups, the religious (monks and nuns) and the laity. Each of these two is clearly defined by rules and responsibilities and by the manner of their mutual interaction which, in turn, serves as a spiritual bond and a traditional basis for close cooperation. The responsibility for preserving and promoting the Buddha's teachings lies in the hands of these two groups of Buddhist followers.

Basic Buddhist systems of worship, including rites and ceremonies, date back to the time of the Buddha. There are, however, later developments which evolved over the centuries in response to the cultural and spiritual needs of the followers in particular geographical regions. Thus, there are differences in the form of worship practised, for instance, in Thailand and Japan. But we may consider this phenomenon a natural cultural manifestation common in all religious systems.

Buddhist sanctuaries are places of worship and residences for the religious. These include monasteries, shrines, Dhamma halls, stupas, pagodas, and sacred reliquaries. Often Thai monasteries, which also serve as centres for communal activities, occasionally do accommodate secular functions such as community meetings and cultural gatherings. In general, these places are built and maintained solely through support freely given by the lay community.

Sacred objects in Buddhism include Buddha images, relics of the Buddha, symbolic representations such as the lotus, the wheel (of Dhamma), Buddha's footprints, and many more. These in fact serve as objects for contemplative reflection and as reminders of higher values or ideals. They can be used to strengthen faith and confidence in the Triple Gem, or to give encouragement and hope in time of distress. On a higher level they may serve as a means for the attainment of Dhamma and that, indeed, is the primary purpose for which they were introduced into the Buddhist institution in the first place.

The above are religious components that constitute Buddhism as an institution. Although the most important factor is the Dhamma, which is man's true refuge, some people may also feel the need for objects of psychological support to strengthen their faith and devotion in the religion. Thus, each component has its own place and value and we should learn how to best benefit from it.

## PHILOSOPHY OR RELIGION?

Strictly speaking, this matter depends largely on how one defines the terms "philosophy" and "religion." Webster's dictionary defines philosophy as "love of wisdom," as "a search for a general understanding of values and reality by chiefly speculative rather than observational means," and religion simply as "the service and worship of God or the supernatural."

One can see that neither of these definitions satisfactorily reflects the nature and character of Buddhism. For many people religion is nothing more than a system of beliefs and worship centered around God. These people would consider any system devoid of such a concept unworthy of inclusion into the category of religions, no matter how exalted a teaching it may contain. This is a rather limited view, no longer accepted by world religions. There are great religious systems that do not subscribe to such a way of thinking.

When the Buddha embarked upon his teaching mission, there was never an issue whether he would establish a religion or found a school of philosophy. Such anticipation was simply out of the question. He had realized the Dhamma, overcome *Saṁsāra*, and achieved Supreme Enlightenment. Foremost in the functions of a Buddha is the exposition of the Dhamma, pointing out the way to lasting peace and happiness for the world. After his enlightenment, he began to share with mankind the supreme knowledge he had attained. There were those willing to listen and who could understand his message. These people benefited from the Buddha's teachings and some of them volunteered to further spread the Dhamma. Others volunteered to provide material support. Those who renounced worldly life became known as *bhikkhus*, collectively referred to as the Saṅgha, and took to the mendicant, homeless life. Householders continued to practise the teachings as laymen or laywomen and took on the responsibility of supporting the Saṅgha. This was how Buddhism evolved and developed. The core factor of all this is the Buddha's teachings, the Dhamma. How people referred to his teachings and the organization that subsequently took shape was never his concern, but he himself referred to the whole structure simply as Dhamma-Vinaya or the Doctrine and Discipline. Clearly, he wanted his teachings to be something that should be properly understood and practised. He wanted the Dhamma-Vinaya to be a way of life.

A way of life—that is exactly what Buddhism is. It is not simply a system of beliefs, or a speculation about values and reality, neither is it the service and worship of God or the supernatural. It is a system of noble principles for man to understand and practise; it is Truth.

Of course, Buddhism has all the necessary components to

qualify as a religion, and there should be no argument on that point, but one should never lose sight of the fact that the Buddhist religion is fundamentally a way of life—something that has to do with life itself and the very heart of existence, not simply "the service and worship of God or the supernatural." (In fact, this can also be said of other religions.)

Not unlike other great religions, Buddhism also contains many different facets to its system. It is possible to view the same Truth from different perspectives, and our opinions about the Truth may vary according to how we look at it. In the same vein, the names that people attach to the system may also differ in accordance with their opinions about it. Thus one may approach Buddhism through its religious or philosophical aspect, or academically attempt to evaluate its ethical relevance in today's social context, according to one's preference. There are also the psychological, literary, cultural, historical, and other aspects of Buddhism that evolved as an outcome of many interacting conditions in the course of history. But valuable as they may seem, these are of secondary significance compared to Buddhism's express role as a way of life.

## THE BUDDHA'S SUCCESSOR

The question of succession was brought up with the Buddha by his personal attendant, Venerable Ānanda, just moments prior to the Great Demise. The Blessed One, however, did not appoint anyone in his place. Instead he advised his followers to regard the doctrine and discipline that he had taught as their teacher. The Dhamma-Vinaya was to succeed him as the highest authority, one from which Buddhists may derive guidance and instruction. This was, indeed, a farsighted proclamation. The Buddha knew that placing absolute powers and responsibility in the hands of any individual could in the long run jeopardize the institution. Even during his lifetime he had made regulatory provisions for the Saṅgha administration to be carried out through collective deliberation and action of its members without vesting any special privileges or prerogatives on any individual. This method remains the model for all ecclesiastical rites and actions within the Saṅgha institution down to the present day.

The fact that the Buddha did not appoint any individual to succeed him is worthy of careful consideration. At the time of his passing away, the Saṅgha had already been firmly established and there were quite a few disciples who were highly accomplished and endowed with superior spiritual attainments. The Buddha would have had no difficulty whatsoever, if he so desired, in naming a suitable successor. But he wisely foresaw that such appointment would set a precedent and, sooner or later, in course of time, some unworthy elements not befitting the lofty position would find their way to the hierarchy. Power, fame, and wealth have, in some intriguing way, a tendency to corrupt otherwise decent people, as is evident in the history of some religions, whose internal power struggles and dirty politics are a matter of astonishment and shame. Buddhist history is relatively free from this kind of pitfall, thanks to the farsightedness of the Buddha.

Secondly, the steps taken by the Buddha at once demonstrate both the philosophy of non-attachment to individuals, which he took pains to emphasize during his mission years, and his explicit trust in the Dhamma as the true refuge in life. At one time the Blessed One admonished a certain monk by the name of Vakkali, who had grown so attached to him that he constantly followed the Buddha wherever he went. The Buddha's words bear the most vivid testimony of his great compassion, utter selflessness, and his desire for the disciple to truly benefit from the Dhamma: "Vakkali, the sight of my person is of no real benefit; whoever sees the Dhamma sees me." It was in this spirit that the Buddha advised his disciples to look up to the Dhamma-Vinaya as his successor. History has more than proved his foresight.

## COMPOSITION OF THE BUDDHIST FOLLOWING

During the time of the Buddha, Buddhist assemblies were divided into four main groups: monks (*bhikkhu*), nuns (*bhikkhunī*), male lay followers (*upāsaka*), and female lay followers (*upāsikā*). In the Theravada tradition the lineage of the Order of Nuns is believed to have terminated about a thousand years after the passing away of the Buddha, so that *bhikkhunīs* in the original sense of the word no longer exist. With an atmosphere of fresh interest and enthusiasm in the religion among Westerners, attempts are being made by certain groups and organizations to revive the *Bhikkhunī* Order in its earlier, pristine form. However, so far the efforts have resulted only in generating some general awareness but still fall short of a complete restoration. Thus, at present we may speak of the Buddhist following in terms of monastic members, which include monks and novices, and the community of laity (both men and women) who profess a belief in the Buddha and his teachings. These are the two major classifications of Buddhists in the Theravada system today.

The Mahayana tradition, however, still maintains the *Bhikkhunī* Order. In those countries where Mahayana Buddhism prevails, such as Vietnam, Korea, and Taiwan, nuns are very much in the forefront where religious affairs and social welfare activities are concerned. They assume strong leadership and contribute greatly to the growth and development of the religion in those lands.

In Theravada tradition monastic members are under strict disciplinary training and are more or less restricted in their social interaction and participation. Nevertheless, they do command faith and respect of the lay community and are well supported in their spiritual endeavor. Monks take upon themselves the express duties of preserving the Dhamma, through study and practice, and teaching it to others. Because of the trust and confidence that people place in them by virtue of their moral integrity and exemplary conduct, they may also provide community leadership where and when their specific services are required. They also give counsel, especially in matters related to religion and spirituality, to the lay community and help maintain peace and harmony in society. But these may be considered natural ramifications of their foremost duties to study and practise the Dhamma, and to attain the highest liberation, which is *Nibbāna*.

Monks and novices lead a different life-style from that of laymen. They live in monasteries in an environment especially structured for scriptural studies and religious training. They follow strict rules of conduct, much more numerous and detailed than those of lay devotees. They sacrifice the life of comfort and pleasure of a layman for the life of austerity and service of a monastic order. Such a sacrifice calls for a deep sense of self-negation, altruism, and compassion. It is a life dedicated to personal enlightenment as well as social well-being.

Despite their different way of life, however, monastic members do not cut themselves off entirely from the mainstream of society. Although social interaction and participation is limited, there is enough to maintain a certain level of cooperation between them and the laity. In Thailand, a strong Buddhist country, the Department of Religious Affairs within the Ministry of Education provides a regular channel of communications between the Saṅgha and the state. His Majesty the King, himself a devout Buddhist, and the Royal Family take a strong interest in religious affairs. They are an important factor for the growth and prosperity of the religion in the country.

## BUDDHISM AND GOD

The concept of God is not common to all religions. Even in theistic religions, ideas about God and his attributes differ from one religious tradition to another, giving rise to conflicts as to whose God is the one and true God. Of course, each claims its God to be the only one, but that has hardly solved the problem.

Buddhism has been defined as a non-theistic religion. Some scholars do not agree with this definition, pointing to Dhamma, the eternally universal principle, as an impersonal God. This is rather a matter of interpretation. But all Buddhists unanimously agree that the Buddha, the Dhamma and the Saṅgha, collectively called the Triple Gem, are the objects of supreme veneration.

The Buddha, the historical personality who lived almost 2,600 years ago, is the founder of the religion; the Dhamma, as the objective manifestation of Truth, is his teachings; and the Saṅgha is the Holy Order of noble disciples who realized the Truth after the Buddha.

As a person, the Buddha is the embodiment of all virtues, having discovered the Dhamma or Truth. One can attain to the same state of enlightenment by walking the path of Dhamma. The Saṅgha are those who have travelled the path of spiritual practice by following the Buddha's teachings, have realized the Dhamma, and are therefore in a position to help others along the same spiritual path.

In essence the Buddha, the Dhamma, and the Saṅgha are one and the same. The sole element that constitutes the quality of being the Buddha and the Saṅgha is none other than the Dhamma itself. Just as a person is not a physician simply on account of his being a person, but rather by virtue of having certain qualities, such as knowledge in medicine and the ability to cure diseases, even so one is not a Buddha because of one's birth into a certain royal family, but rather on the condition of having attained the quality of Buddha-hood, which is the Dhamma. The same is true with regard to the Saṅgha, the difference being that the Buddha was the first to discover the Dhamma, while the Saṅgha became enlightened by walking the spiritual path after him.

It was the Buddha who first realized the Dhamma and taught it to the world. But without the Dhamma, Buddhahood could not be attained. Again there would not be the Saṅgha without the Buddha and the Dhamma. But without the Saṅgha, the Buddha and the Dhamma would be of little value to the world and the religion would not have been established; even if it were, it would have died out with the death of the Buddha. The three are thus interrelated and interdependent.

## WORSHIP IN BUDDHISM

Like the term 'religion,' the meaning of the word 'worship' as generally understood is rather limited and should be redefined. According to Webster's dictionary, worship is "reverence offered a divine being or supernatural power" or "an act of expressing such reverence." All religious traditions have a system of worship in some form or another, and it is generally accepted as constituting an act of faith, or an expression thereof, toward the so-called divine being or supernatural power. This is not worship in Buddhism.

In Buddhism, worship is an expression of respect and gratitude to the Triple Gem. It is an act of veneration offered to that which is worthy, not a prayer or a gesture of submission to a supernatural being. Thus, although Buddha images are used in worship, idolatry is a practice not encouraged in Buddhism. The Buddhist concept of worship is totally different from that of idol worship. Its nature is more of a spiritual practice rather than a mere exercise in faith and devotion, although such elements are also present in the practice.

Fundamentally, there are three advantages derived from an act of Buddhist worship, in addition to the obvious benefit of fortifying faith in the Triple Gem. First, the practice helps to inspire virtues and inculcates the noble qualities associated with the Triple Gem into the mind. Wholesome qualities such as wisdom, compassion, and purity are essential in all spiritual efforts. Second, the act of worship has a deep purifying effect on the devotees' consciousness and the power to remove impurities from their minds. Often, a sense of serenity and peace is produced. Third, Buddhist worship can be performed as a meditative exercise for developing concentration and wisdom. Prayer for material gains and success is, therefore, never part of true Buddhist worship, as it would prove an obstacle to the development of these two important qualities of mind. Undue desire for material objectives is based on greed and selfishness and is likely to cause mental disturbance, frustration, and restlessness, which are impurities of the mind. Worship performed with the right attitude can be of great benefit; like all other actions, it should be based on wisdom and understanding.

## CULTURAL ADAPTATIONS

Just as in other ancient religions, Buddhism has been subject to various forces and developments through the centuries of its existence. Because it spread to countries far beyond the boundaries of its birthplace, Buddhism has come into contact with varying cultural elements and geographical conditions. In response to those influences, the religion has developed into different denominations, with their own distinct characteristics. Some of these seemingly different traditions continue to prosper and are more widely accepted in some countries or regions than others. Theravada Buddhism, for instance, is chiefly practised in Thailand, Burma, Sri Lanka, Cambodia, Laos, and certain parts of India and Bangladesh, while Mahayana Buddhism is followed in such countries as Japan, Korea, China, Tibet, Taiwan, Vietnam, and Singapore.

However, if one takes a closer look at the many different Buddhist traditions that exist today, one will immediately see that most of those apparent differences come within two categories.

First, there are the external modifications, like dress, ways of worship, and mannerisms, necessitated by the different elements and cultures that Buddhism had been exposed to. Second, there are the differences in emphasis given by each tradition to certain aspects of the teaching. For example, the Theravada tradition is characterized by the stress it places on monastic discipline, while Mahayana Buddhism upholds the Bodhisattva ideal. Some Mahayana traditions also greatly emphasize the importance of vegetarianism. All this may create the impression that Buddhist traditions are in opposition to each other, but such an understanding is not well grounded.

As far as the essence and spirit of the teachings are concerned, there are persistent and uniform characteristics among the many Buddhist traditions that are far more significant and enduring than the superficial differences. Despite the outward diversity, underneath it lies the eternal unity of all Buddhist denominations, based on the Buddha's message of wisdom and compassion.

## BUDDHISM AND MATERIAL DEVELOPMENT

It is often thought that to lead the life of Dhamma is one thing and to be materially successful is quite another. According to this view, to progress materially one must relentlessly pursue the worldly course without any consideration whatsoever of the Dhamma, and to lead a life of Dhamma one must be ready to renounce the world and retire to a forest or a cave. The image of the Dhamma practitioner never quite seems to fit into a worldly context and he is often viewed as something of an anachronism. This kind of misunderstanding exists not only among the unlettered—even the educated are led to such conclusions. It is an unfortunate misconception based on a lack of knowledge on the Dhamma.

To avoid this pitfall, students of the Dhamma should learn to perceive the relationship between the Dhamma and the world. In fact, there is no Dhamma apart from the world, and no world apart from the Dhamma. The dualistic view separating one from the other may lead to confusion and deleterious results, while a correct attitude will lead to true happiness and progress. For instance, if nuclear energy is developed without cultivating a sense of moral responsibility to direct the use of that technology, it is likely that more harm than benefit will result from it. Power and wealth without Dhamma create fear and insecurity. Greed may motivate the acquisition of more wealth, but it will also cause pain and misery, thus rendering the whole process of acquisition meaningless.

Those who uphold the dualistic view often perceive the Dhamma as an obstacle to material development and progress. A businessman with such a philosophy will do anything to make more profits for himself and his company; a politician with the same outlook will strive to gain more and more power, through means fair and foul; a teenager with this misconception would go out of his way to pursue carnal pleasure and excitement just to gratify his senses. In all these cases, there is no place for the Dhamma; such people would see practising the Dhamma as an obstacle to achieving their desired objectives.

However, with right understanding, we will see that the Dhamma is truly the basis for real progress, even in material concerns. Perseverance, energy, dedication to work, to name a few, are important qualities that are essential for success even in the pursuit of material ambitions. With kindness and compassion, those ambitions can be transformed from tools for selfish satisfaction to actions which benefit fellow beings in society and bear a lasting testimony of one's virtue. A politician who practices Dhamma will turn his power and energy and the people's trust into an instrument for peace, social justice, and further progress, rather than using them for his own selfish gains. A scientist with a heart of Dhamma will endeavor to make sure that his discoveries or inventions enhance well-being and happiness for the world rather than destruction and suffering. A Dhamma practitioner who perceives the unity of the world and the Dhamma will not be content merely to cultivate passive love and compassion, but will ensure that such noble qualities of heart are translated into action that will benefit the world. He does not run away from the world simply to practise Dhamma for its own sake, but will try to make Dhamma grow in the world, and the world in the Dhamma. Thus Dhamma and the world are perceived in a balanced way as the Buddha intended.

External progress, according to Buddhism, must therefore be coupled with internal development. In other words, material progress must be accompanied by spiritual development; the practice of Dhamma should be directed toward active service to society. Other than the necessary requisites, we also need moral values, good ethics and a sense of responsibility.

## BECOMING A BUDDHIST

Technically speaking, to take refuge in the Buddha, the Dhamma, and the Saṅgha constitutes being a Buddhist. This can be done either by making a conscious, non-ceremonial commitment to the Triple Gem, or by going through a ceremony officiated by a Buddhist monk. During the time of the Buddha we hear of people, sometimes as many as hundreds or thousands, who, having been inspired by a discourse from the Buddha, made declarations of faith in the Triple Gem, becoming followers of the Buddha without any special ceremony. In any case, the most important factor is a willingness to practise according to the Buddha's teachings and to lead the life of a Buddhist. In the *Aṅguttara Nikāya*,* the Buddha talks about five qualities of a good Buddhist:

_____

*One of the books of the Suttanta Piṭaka, the Collection of Discourses, of the Buddhist Pali Canon.

confidence and faith in the Triple Gem; being well-trained in moral conduct; faith in *kamma* (one's actions), never in superstition; not seeking a 'field of merits' outside the Buddha's teachings; and paying constant attention to the prosperity of Buddhism.

Fundamental to all Buddhists is the observance of the five precepts, which enjoin against killing, stealing, sexual misconduct, falsehood, and intoxicants. Breaking a precept negatively affects the quality of one's status as a Buddhist. The transgressed precepts may be 'renewed' by making a fresh commitment to the moral practice or by formally renewing one's commitment to them in the presence of a monk. The precepts are intended to be a course of training in morality and a support for the practice of Dhamma.

There are a large number of men and women in the West today who are appreciative of Buddhism, but are not yet ready to call themselves Buddhists. Most of these people are interested in finding a religious alternative and a more meaningful way of life. They discover in Buddhist teachings something that can answer their intellectual curiosity and satisfy their spiritual needs, and so they are willing to practise the religion in their daily life. One such person was Professor Rhys Davids, a renowned British scholar, who openly admitted: "I have examined every one of the great religions of the world, and in none of them have I found anything to surpass the beauty and comprehensiveness of the Four Noble Truths of the Buddha. I am content to shape my life according to them."

Of course, Davids is a Buddhist, but there are many Westerners like him who practise the religion without formally identifying themselves with it. They also benefit from the Buddha's teachings. The Dhamma is universal; it transcends all limitations of time and space. It makes no distinction in terms of sex, nationality, the color of the skin, social status, or belief. It is open to all. Its validity does not depend on names, titles, or professions, neither is it restricted by temporal or spatial conditions.

The Dhamma can, therefore, be practised by all people with

sufficient intellectual and spiritual maturity to understand it. However, taking refuge in the Triple Gem and consciously culti-vating the identity of being a Buddhist can provide a tremendous moral support, helping to sustain one's confidence and effort through the ups and downs of the practice and providing a religious inspiration for walking in the steps of the Buddha with stronger faith and commitment.

# 3

# THE BUDDHA

THE BUDDHA IS BELIEVED TO HAVE BEEN born around the year 623 BC (although some traditions put the date at 563 BC) on the Nepalese side of what is now the border of India and Nepal. His father was King Suddhodhana, his mother Queen Maya, and the capital city from where they reigned was Kapilavatthu, a Himalayan Kingdom in the north of India.

In his early years the Buddha was known by the name Siddhattha Gotama (Sanskrit: Siddhartha Gautama) and it was predicted that he would either become a universal monarch or a great religious teacher. Many wondrous miracles are said to have accompanied the prince's birth. However, his mother died seven days after he was born and he was thereafter brought up by Pajāpati, his aunt and foster mother. Siddhattha showed signs of greatness from his early childhood. He was kind, compassionate, and extremely intelligent. His love was known to extend to all living creatures and his wisdom was extraordinary. He was, indeed, destined to become a great personality whose life would affect humanity as a whole.

The King, of course, wanted the young prince to succeed him to the throne. He saw to it that his promising son was married to a beautiful princess from a neighboring state. But Siddhattha would not be tied down forever to the family life and worldly concerns. Eventually, at the age of twenty-nine, he bade farewell to his family, the throne, and the kingdom to become an ascetic in search of Truth and enlightenment. He practised with many renowned teachers and experimented with various severe austerities, but none of them impressed him as the right way to ultimate realization of the Truth. He started to practice meditation on his own, using his own methods, determined, unguided and unsupported by others.

Six years after the Great Renunciation, alone in the deep jungles of northern India, Siddhattha became enlightened. The Dhamma had been realized and the end of the search had been reached. From now on he became known as the Buddha, the Enlightened One or the Awakened One. He started to teach the Dhamma to the world. The first discourse was delivered to a group of five ascetics, who became his followers. Soon more and more people came to join him and they helped to spread the teaching.

The Buddha worked hard for forty-five years bringing his noble message to the world. His fame spread far and wide, attracting more and more followers to him. A monastic Order came into existence and rapidly expanded; the Saṅgha members further helped him in his mission to bring the Dhamma to an even wider audience. Support and following came from people in all walks of life: kings and queens, princes and princesses, ministers, army chiefs, soldiers, bureaucrats, physicians, entertainers, traders, workers, farmers, peasants, prostitutes, and beggars—practically from all classes and segments in society. The spread of the Dhamma during the Buddha's time was a spiritual revolution, a large scale social reform, and a unique phenomenon in the history of religions. By the time he passed away in the year 543 BC, at the age of eighty, the religion had already been firmly established.

After the death of the Buddha, his noble disciples continued the task of spreading the Dhamma. In course of time, some two centuries later, the Buddhist influence began to extend far beyond the boundaries of its birth-place. During the reign of Emperor Ashoka, the religion was even introduced to the lands of the Greeks in the west, Sri Lanka in the south, and Suvaṇṇabhumi (Thailand) in the east. Emperors Kanishka and Harshawardhana were two other monarchs in ancient India who were instrumental in promoting Buddhism in the empire and its further spread in foreign lands.

## THE BUDDHA AND MIRACLES

Eastern traditions often associate extraordinary events with the birth of a great personality. The birth of some kings in ancient times, for instance, is reported to have been attended by such wondrous phenomena as unseasonal rainstorms, lightning and thunder, and sudden outbursts of brilliant light from no apparent source. These events were seen as prophetic signs, indicating the greatness of the person whose birth was taking place at the time. It is possible that as time passed certain legends might have evolved around those wonders. Literary records have a marked tendency to add liberal servings of imagination and decoration. This kind of practice was, in fact, more or less universal in earlier days.

The birth of the Buddha was undoubtedly a unique event in the history of mankind. It is not improbable that certain unusual phenomena might have taken place, which were construed to indicate his greatness and the mission that lay ahead. The Buddha himself paid little attention to such things. Unlike some religions that depend heavily on miracles to substantiate their teachings, Buddhism needed no miracles to glorify its founder's position. In fact, the Buddha discouraged his disciples from being attached to miracles or miraculous powers. For him, the miracle of the Dhamma is the greatest miracle of all, one that we can all achieve and see for ourselves, and in fact is the only miracle that can be of any real benefit to our lives.

Buddhist commentaries describe at great length the many miracles reported to have attended the birth of the Buddha. He was born at Lumbini Park on the full moon of the sixth lunar month. Deities from all heavenly realms came to welcome him and pay reverence. Even eminent gods like Brahma and Indra were there to express their joy at his birth. Heavenly music filled the air and two showers, one hot and one cold, came down from the sky to bathe the child. The earth trembled and the heavenly beings gave out loud acclaims of joy.

It is also said that, immediately after his birth, the infant stood firmly on the ground and took seven strides to the north, surrounded by gods and men. A white canopy was held over his head. Having walked the seven steps, he stopped to look around and gave out a fearless utterance known as the 'lion's roar' (*sihanāda*). His proclamation may be translated as follows:

> Supreme am I in the world;
> Greatest am I in the world;
> Noblest am I in the world.
> This is my last birth,
> Never shall I be reborn.

It is possible that the miracles accompanying the Buddha's birth described in the early commentaries may point to something deeper and more meaningful. Early writers were prone to use such symbolic descriptions to explain certain Dhamma principles, but in later times their true intentions and meanings have become so obscured that an interpretative enquiry is required in order to reveal the real spirit of those cryptic expressions. Thus the baby's standing on the ground is interpreted as his being well established in the four Virtues of Accomplishment (*iddhipāda*—aspiration, effort, mental application and reasoning); turning northward means the spiritual conquest of the multitudes; the seven steps signify the seven Factors of Enlightenment (*bojjhaṅga*—mindfulness, investigation of Dhamma, effort, rapture, calmness, concentration, equanimity); the white canopy suggests the spread of Dhamma that brings peace to the world; looking around indicates the seeing and unveiling of supreme knowledge; the fearlessness of the lion's roar denotes the utter success in proclaiming the Dhamma; and the last birth means the attainment of Arahantship. This is another way of looking at unusual events described in some Buddhist literature, an interpretative approach, aimed at discovering a deeper meaning in the narration of what may seem extraordinary events beyond our normal range of comprehension.

It is said that the birth of all Buddhas, past, present, and future, is accompanied by miracles. A question is often asked if, in fact, such miracles do occur. Answering "Yes" or "No" would mean the same for sceptics. Believers, of course, find no need to ask such questions: if extraordinary things, like escaping unscathed from dangerous accidents, can happen to an ordinary worldling, they argue, why could something very extraordinary not happen to so great a personality as the Buddha? For Buddhists, however, there is no controversy, as there is complete freedom to accept or deny such matters. Since the Buddha said that miracles are capable of misleading one from the path of Dhamma, we should take a realistic view of the matter and not be attached to them. If they were essential for the attainment of Nibbāna, or if they were conducive to real benefit, the Buddha would have encouraged us to pay greater attention to them. On the contrary, the Buddha on more than one occasion warned his disciples not to be attached to miracles. He even forbade his monks from performing them to attract attention. There is a grave penalty imposed on monks who boast of having higher powers (to perform miracles, for example) that they do not possess. From the Buddhist perspective, miracles are therefore not an important factor in the practice of Dhamma.

45

## MORAL IMPLICATIONS OF THE BUDDHA'S RENUNCIATION

There are men who walk out on their families for selfish reasons, but such actions are irresponsible and cannot be condoned. Prince Siddhattha was known for his compassion and kindness. Certainly, he did not leave his family and everything behind for selfish reasons. He renounced the life of abundance and pleasure for a life of poverty and austerity. He gave up the prospective throne with all the attending ministers and state dignitaries to live in jungles among wild birds and beasts. He sacrificed wealth and power to lead the life of an ascetic, penniless and alone. No one could accuse Siddhattha of having left his family and country for the sake of pleasure and sensual gratification. His decision was based on compassionate altruism; it was an act of sacrifice and farsightedness.

It is said that Siddhattha's life in the palaces was one of abundant luxury and constant pleasure. His father, apprehensive that the young prince would one day leave home to become an ascetic, had made certain that he was well provided for and would thereby be attached to the worldly life. But Siddhattha saw through the illusion of worldly pleasures, transitory and unsatisfactory as they were; he knew no sorrow, but he felt profoundly touched by the sorrow of humanity. Still in the prime of his youth, enjoying physical strength and good health, he perceived the inexorable nature of life and the universal sickness of humanity. Amidst luxury and comfort, he contemplated the universality of suffering to which all beings are subjected. His innate compassion would not allow him to selfishly enjoy the pleasures and privileges of royalty. The world was full of conflict and confusion, plagued by violence and oppression, and Siddhattha wanted to find a way to overcome these sufferings. His act of going forth from home to homelessness is known as the Great Renunciation; it was a great sacrifice for the benefit of the whole of humanity.

Siddhattha's position may be better understood through an analogy: when a country's sovereignty is threatened by an enemy, it is the duty of the soldiers of that country to respond. There may be some able-bodied young men who would rather remain home and let others fight for the country, but a brave and duty-conscious soldier would willingly choose to leave home, his wife, family, and everything else in order to be on the battlefield. No one could accuse him of being irresponsible to his wife and family; his leaving home is considered a great sacrifice for the sake of the country and his fellow countrymen.

In the same way, Siddhattha could have elected to remain in the royal household and enjoy the wealth, privileges, and power befitting a prince, but he decided to leave home to do what all the authority and wealth that were at his command could not do. In the process he had to undergo great hardship and personal discomfort. But the Dhamma he discovered and taught to the world has brought peace and happiness to countless people over the centuries, and is still of great benefit to humanity today. Had he chosen to lead a household life and ascend the throne following his father, his services to mankind would have been much more limited.

Siddhattha's decision to leave home could not have been an easy one. He had a young son, a loving wife, a concerned father and foster mother, and a promising future of power and glory. He also knew all too well that the austere life of an ascetic was one of great hardship, loneliness, and discomfort—so completely different from the one he was enjoying. It must have taken great courage, determination, and selfless sacrifice to arrive at this crucial decision and not to waver in his resolve.

Six years later, after undergoing untold suffering and hardship, Siddhattha accomplished what he had set out to do. Like a victorious soldier, he returned to the world and began to expound the Dhamma he had realized through his own determination and effort. He even visited his father and family and taught them to realize the Dhamma. Many in the royal household joined the

Order, including his former wife, his son, and foster mother, who all attained the highest bliss of *Nibbāna*.

## MANY BUDDHAS

The question concerning the status of Buddhahood is yet another positive indication of how accommodating and straightforward Buddhism is. The Buddha never claimed a monopoly or prerogative over Buddhahood, nor did he ever make an attempt to discourage others from attaining to it. Inspired by his personality and his achievement, many were even tempted to aspire for the exalted position of Buddhahood and made such declarations before him.

The word Buddha is a generic term, meaning the Enlightened One. It refers to a person who has realized the Dhamma and attained enlightenment. This enlightenment, as we have seen, is open to all, and so is Buddhahood. In line with the Theravada teachings, Mahayana tradition goes a step further to strongly assert the universal presence of Buddha-nature in all beings, without exception; this Buddha-nature is the inherent potential for enlightenment, which can be cultivated and actualized by each and every individual. This spirit of openness and tolerance is characteristic of Buddhism.

As far as attaining enlightenment is concerned, Theravada literature describes three kinds of Buddhas. One who has attained supreme and complete enlightenment through his own efforts, unaided and unguided, and is capable of teaching the truth he has realized to others, is known as *Sammāsambuddha,* the Perfectly Self-Enlightened One. The second kind of Buddha is the one who has, likewise, attained enlightenment (through his own effort and without any external assistance) but is incapable of imparting his knowledge to others in such a way that they also could realize the Dhamma. He is known as *Paccekabuddha* or Silent Buddha. The third category, added by the commentaries, consists of those who attain enlightenment not solely through their own effort, but through the guidance and assistance of a *Sammāsambuddha*. These are known as *Anubuddhas* or *Sāvakabuddhas*. Some Mahayana authors prefer to call *Anubuddhas*, or those people with exceptional knowledge and spiritual experience, simply *buddhas* (small 'b'). Theravada tradition popularly refers to those noble disciples, who have realized the Truth after the *Sammāsambuddha* and have achieved the highest stage of spiritual attainment, as *Arahants*.

In the Theravada tradition, when we use the term Buddha (always with a capital B), we specifically refer to a *Sammāsambuddha*, especially to Gotama, the historical Buddha who was born in 623 BC and who founded the Buddhist religion in its present dispensation. During the period when the world is void of a Buddha or a Buddhist dispensation, there may be many individuals who realize the Dhamma and become *Paccekabuddhas*. Once a *Sammāsambuddha* attains enlightenment and begins his religious dispensation, all those who realize *Nibbāna* through his teachings are known as *Anubuddhas*. This applies throughout the whole length of that particular dispensation.

The attainment of the status of *Sammāsambuddha* or *Paccekabuddha* is said to be in accordance with a resolution made in the past and the fulfillment of ten Perfections. These are generosity (*dāna*), morality (*sīla*), renunciation (*nekkhamma*), wisdom (*paññā*), forbearance (*khanti*), truthfulness (*sacca*), resolution (*adhiṭṭhāna*), loving-kindness (*mettā*), and equanimity (*upekkhā*). However, the experience of *Nibbāna* is the same, differences among individuals lying chiefly in their abilities to expound the Dhamma and the extent to which they can help free others from *Saṁsāra* and lead them to the other shore of *Nibbāna*.

# THE BODHISATTVA

*Bodhisattva* is a Sanskrit term, the equivalent Pali term being *Bodhisatta*. Originally, the term may have been used in reference to all beings who aspire to attain enlightenment. Thus, one who practises in order to realize *Nibbāna* is called a *Bodhisattva*.

Technically, however, the term *Bodhisattva* is used in the Theravada tradition exclusively in connection with an aspirant who strives to be a *Sammāsambuddha*. The most important factor to qualify one as a *Bodhisattva* is the prophetic pronouncement, made in person by a Buddha, confirming the future fulfillment of the aspirant's resolve to strive for Buddhahood. So long as the aspirant has not received such a prophesy, it is possible that he may lapse from his original resolution and give up his efforts, which is the case with most individuals. The Buddha's prophesy is the surest guarantee that a person will one day achieve Buddhahood, no matter how long or how many lifetimes it will take. From the moment he receives the Buddha's assurance until the moment he attains the supreme enlightenment in his last existence, he is known throughout as a *Bodhisattva,* and nothing can discourage or divert him from his goal. It is not uncommon that a *Bodhisattva* receives confirmation from other Buddhas from time to time, in different dispensations, during the unimaginably long course of wandering through Saṁsāra before he attains *Nibbāna.* Our Buddha is said to have received such confirmation from no less than twenty-four Buddhas.

To be entitled to the first confirmation, an individual must be spiritually advanced to the extent that, if he so wishes, he could attain Arahantship in that very life. He must also be endowed with special attainments, such as *jhāna* (higher stages of concentration), and must make a declaration of his resolve before a Buddha. It is said that, having heard the aspirant's declaration, that Buddha will look into the future with the infinite power of his omniscience, and make a proper pronouncement. Gotama the Buddha received his first prophesy from the Buddha Dīpankara. He was then known as Sumedha and was leading the life of an ascetic, highly advanced in spiritual maturity and psychic powers. Although he possessed the capacity to attain Arahantship in that very life, yet he postponed his final attainment of Nibbāna and, out of his concern for the happiness and liberation of all creatures, made a determined aspiration for Buddhahood.

The point to be noted here is the willful postponement of Arahantship. Clearly, this involves great sacrifice and altruism. Instead of gaining the final liberation and attaining the ultimate bliss of Nibbāna, a Bodhisattva wilfully volunteers to prolong his sojourn in Saṁsāra so that he may further cultivate and expand his capacity to help other beings; he puts others' interests before his own and is willing to suffer for their sake. This is the essential spirit of all Bodhisattvas.

There are certain qualities that must be fully cultivated by a Bodhisattva before he can realize Buddhahood. These are the ten Perfections mentioned above. During the long sojourn in Saṁsāra, a Bodhisattva may take birth in different planes of existence, according to his kamma, but he will not be born in eighteen inauspicious states, for instance being born blind, deaf, insane, an idiot, crippled, in the womb of a slave, or as a heretic. He will not be born in the lowest hell or among the hungry ghosts, neither will he be born in the Formless Realms. Although he is still liable to commit wrong deeds, there are five evil actions that he would never do. These are called the five Immediacy-Crimes, namely, matricide, patricide, the killing of an Arahant, causing a Buddha to suffer a wound, and creating a schism in the Sangha.

The length of Bodhisattvas' wanderings in Saṁsāra differs according to the three qualities of wisdom (paññā), faith (saddhā), and perseverance (viriya), in which each wishes to attain eminence. While still a Bodhisattva, Gotama the Buddha excelled in the quality of wisdom, which helps shorten the time required to fulfill the ten Perfections. Those Bodhisattvas who wish to excel in the other two qualities take a much longer time, but travel a relatively smoother course, to achieve the same goal. In their penultimate life all *Bodhisattvas* are born in Tusita heaven before taking the last birth in the human world. Once enlightened, all Buddhas are equally endowed with regard to their omniscience, psychic powers, knowledge of the Dhamma, and experience of *Nibbāna*. All Buddhas teach exactly the same Dhamma to the world.

## THE BUDDHA'S DAILY ROUTINE

Canonical literature uses the term *lokatthacariyā* to describe the Buddha's duties throughout his years of mission as the Buddha. Literally, it means conduct for the welfare of the world. It is a rather general description, but it is really what the Buddha did until his very last breath. The later commentaries added *ñātatthacariyā*, conduct for the welfare of his relatives, and *buddhatthacariyā*, beneficial conduct constituting the duty of a Buddha.

The Buddha's day was well organized and carefully structured. He divided the third watch of the night (2 a.m.–6 a.m.—according to ancient Indian usage, a night had three equal parts, each with a duration of four hours) into three parts: the first part he spent in ambulatory meditation, the second in sleep, and the third in another session of meditation, during which he surveyed the world with his divine eye in order to see if there were beings who would benefit from a visit that day.

Each day, early in the morning, the Buddha would put on his robes and go for almsround (*piṇḍapāta*), giving others an opportunity to accrue merits by offering food to him. If there were people who would benefit from his presence, he would make it a point to pay them a visit, even if it meant travelling long distances, and give them some appropriate discourse. Sometimes, he walked alone or with a few other monks; sometimes he was accompanied by a large following. After the meal, which was the only one for the day, he returned to his residence.

The next function he performed was giving advice to monks. Those who wished to receive instruction in meditation could do so at this time. The Buddha also answered questions brought up by his monks and delivered discourses appropriate to the occasion. Having done that, he retired to his cell and, if he wished, spent some time in restful solitude. Then he would again survey the world with his clairvoyance to see if anyone needed his presence and instruction. Those who were spiritually mature enough to benefit from his instruction would appear before his divine vision and he would take appropriate steps to fulfill their spiritual needs.

The Buddha bathed in the evening. After his bath, he began his first watch session of the night, attending to monks who came to seek advice for their practice and giving them discourses. The middle watch was an opportunity for deities and other beings to seek his audience and advice. Often, kings, princes, or ministers, who had no time during the day, would avail themselves of this opportunity. The last watch of the night was spent as mentioned above; in this same watch the Buddha meditated, slept, arose, attended to his physical needs, and "cast the net of his divine vision" to select those whom he would teach.

Except during *Vassa* (Rains Retreat), the Blessed One was always on the move, delivering discourses and giving advice to the masses. But even when he was travelling, he kept up the usual routines, working hard to fulfill his duties as 'the teacher of gods and men.'

## BUDDHA AND DIVINE INTERVENTION

Buddhism is a man-centered religion. The Buddha claimed to be no more than a human being and he taught that a human being, and only a human being, is capable of the highest spiritual attainment. His supreme enlightenment, his achievement in

53

spiritual perfection, was the result of his own efforts and had nothing to do with divine intervention. Neither was it inspired by divine authority. The Buddha never claimed to be God's prophet or messenger.

During the Buddha's time, belief in God was quite prevalent. In fact, many gods and goddesses were worshipped. At the head of all these deities was Brahma the Creator, the Supreme Godhead who created the universe and everything in it. The Buddha considered all deities merely as sentient beings in different planes of existence, subject, like man, to the laws of change and impermanence. The Buddha was quite unequivocal in his rejection of the concept of a creator God. All things are, according to Buddhism, interrelated and interdependent; everything arises and disappears according to the law of conditionality. A creator God is, therefore, an impossible and illogical proposition.

The Buddha was a man, universally respected by men and gods because of his unsurpassed spiritual perfection. In that respect he was more divine than any divinity, and superior to all beings. He taught that all beings are capable of attaining the same high state of spiritual development that he himself had reached by following the path of Dhamma he had shown. The Buddha is like a seasoned traveller who, after a long and arduous journey, has reached the destination and has come to show the way to others.

## THE UNIQUE QUALITIES OF A BUDDHA

Rather than worshipping the Buddha as a God or deity, Buddhists worship him as one would pay respect to a great teacher. This helps to inculcate in our minds the qualities of peace, joy, and humility, qualities that are equally valued in all religious traditions. While in the act of worship, reflecting on the Buddha's virtues of universal compassion, perfect purity, and boundless wisdom inspires our hearts to make an effort to lead a life according to those spiritual qualities. When we look at the Buddha statue in a shrine, with its benevolent smile and eyes cast down in a gesture of inner tranquillity, we feel peaceful and happy, and are spontaneously reminded of higher spiritual attainments to aspire to.

What are sometimes referred to as Buddhist prayers, recited in ceremony or worship, are not prayers at all; Buddhists do not pray. What they recite, individually or in groups, are Pali passages that contain the Buddha's teachings. Each time we recite those passages, we reflect on the noble message of the Buddha so that we may be inspired to put it into practice in our daily life. Even the flowers on the altar can be a teaching: they demonstrate to us the ephemeral nature of life and the inherent unsatisfactoriness of all things. Such a reflection helps to reveal an aspect of reality that may otherwise elude our perception.

Thus, when we bow down before the Buddha image, we are simply expressing our deep sense of gratitude to a great teacher who has given so much to the world. But for his enduring contribution, the world would not have seen such a spiritual treasure.

## THE BUDDHA AFTER DEATH

The Buddha often declared that without realization of the Dhamma, one cannot be said to have seen the Buddha. The statement implies that in essence the real Buddha is none other than the Dhamma. This real Buddha is therefore eternal, not subject to old age and death. In his physical form the Buddha was only human and was subject to the normal conditions of existence just as anybody else. The physical form was necessary for the expression of the Dhamma, which is the real Buddha, but, like anything else that exists, it must finally come to an end. In other words, we may say that the physical form was only the temporary manifestation of the real Buddha, which is eternal and not subject to old age and death.

If we understand the meaning of the Buddha's statement, then we will clearly see that the real Buddha did not, and will not, die at all. What passed away more than 2,500 years ago was merely the physical form of someone called Prince Siddhattha, who became enlightened and was thereafter known as the Buddha, and who, like anyone else, was subject to the laws of impermanence, unsatisfactoriness, and non-substantiality. That physical structure, together with its bodily and mental functions, was part of nature; it existed and operated according to the laws of nature.

The real Buddha still lives among us, in our hearts. If we practise the Dhamma, we will see the real Buddha in all his glory and splendor. We only derive real benefit from the Buddha when we earnestly practise according to his teaching. That is how the real Buddha benefits us, or, to use a theistic expression, how he answers our prayers. It is the most significant and meaningful way to answer prayers, for the benefit of the Dhamma can be experienced immediately in an objective way. All that is required is an open mind and the intellectual maturity to understand it.

Those who claim that God answers their prayers do so out of sheer faith, although they have difficulty understanding God's nature or proving his existence. Ultimately, they have to resort to blind faith, claiming God's omnipotence and unpredictable nature. But blind faith is something that the Buddha openly discouraged. Buddhists are relatively free from that kind of difficulty because the Dhamma, which is the real Buddha, is something that can be directly experienced, understood, and practised.

When the Buddha declared on his deathbed that he wished his disciples to look to the Dhamma-Vinaya as their teacher, he was in fact referring to the real Buddha in the most objective form, and appointing that as his 'successor.' Buddhists are therefore never without the protection and guidance of the real Buddha, which is, in essence, the eternal Dhamma.

## Different kinds of Buddha

Just as a single object can be viewed differently from different angles, the Buddha can be understood differently by different people, depending on the intellectual or spiritual capacities of each individual. A small child, for instance, when asked to identify the Buddha, may point to a Buddha image and say, "That's the Buddha." Older people may laugh at such naivete and say that the Buddha was a man who lived and taught in India more than 2,500 years ago. This is the Buddha that most people know and refer to. There is nothing wrong with such a perception—the Buddha is a historical personality, someone who actually lived and worked and brought about a spiritual upheaval in the history of religions—but those who are spiritually more mature would perceive that the real Buddha, on a metaphysical level, is the Dhamma itself. They understand that the realization of the Dhamma amounts to the seeing of the real Buddha.

It is interesting to note that the Buddha is also known by a number of other names, among which is 'Dhammakāya,' the Dhamma-body or the Embodiment of Dhamma. Clearly, this indicates the true essence of the Buddha and how the Dhamma finds its manifest form in the Buddha. This Dhammakāya, it must be pointed out, is inherent in all of us. Some have been able to realize it and become enlightened; others may not be aware of its existence and pay no attention to it. This is the Buddha-nature that is within us all the time, and it is up to each and every individual to realize. Consider this statement made to the Buddha by the nun Pajāpati, who had been his foster mother, and later his Arahant disciple: "Lord, I am your mother and you are my father. Your physical form did I develop and bring to growth, whereas my blissful Dhamma-body you cultivated to perfection." The distinction and relationship between the historical Buddha as an objective manifestation of Dhamma on the one hand, and the real Buddha as the very essence of the Dhamma on the other, can be clearly seen in this declaration.

## PROSTRATING AND IDOLATRY

The first Buddha image came into existence long after the Buddha passed away. It is one of the many objects that Buddhists use for concentration practice or as a point of focus to reflect on the Buddha and his virtues. It reminds them of the greatest man who ever lived and inspires them to follow his example in their efforts on the spiritual path.

Popular Buddhism treats Buddha images as sacred objects because they symbolize higher values and ideals. Buddhists show respect to the Buddha by bowing down or making a gesture of obeisance before a Buddha image. Sometimes they even believe that there are special powers associated with certain images. This is just another example of different levels of understanding with regard to Buddha images.

With right understanding and proper attitude, a Buddha image becomes a vehicle for the increase of virtues and an instrument for spiritual growth. It is never an act of idolatry, which is defined as "the worship of a physical object as a god." This definition is quite antithetic to the nature and spirit of worship in Buddhism. Those who properly understand Buddhism and Buddhist practice will realize that there is no place for idolatry in the religion. Bowing down before a Buddha image is an act of piety, an expression of humble respect and gratitude for the Buddha; it is a simple gesture that helps to purify the mind and transform character in accordance with Buddhist ideals. Such an act may be regarded as a Dhamma practice.

It is interesting to note that the Buddha himself said: "Driven by fear, the multitudes go for refuge to mountains, forests, trees, and shrines. Such are not safe or supreme refuges. Having gone to such refuges, one is not free from suffering (*dukkha*)."

The same can be said of the greed and ignorance that drive people to make wishes to supposedly sacred or supernaturally endowed objects. Such objects can be anything, animate as well as inanimate, and may even include animals. Cows are sacred animals in India, and so are monkeys and snakes. But we may take it from the Buddha that such objects are not safe or supreme refuges. We cannot be free from problems by worshipping such objects.

Although some Buddhists may be seen offering prayers and making wishes, that kind of superstitious indulgence does not have any basis in the Buddhist teaching. Such practices have their origin more in popular superstition and misunderstanding. At best they may have resulted from the Buddhist interaction with other religions or cultures. In any case, such practices cannot be cited as a standard for judging or evaluating the religion because they lack doctrinal support.

To be fair, praying and wish-making are superstitions that have been practised since time immemorial, and will continue to be practised as long as people have not grasped the real meaning and essence of the Dhamma. To be free from this kind of superstition, man needs to cultivate self-confidence and moral strength, based on a clear understanding of the law of *kamma*. Meanwhile, the practice may have some short-term psychological benefit and may provide temporary relief for those who cherish blind faith and false hope.

Wishes based on wisdom and made without selfish motives are by no means superstitious acts. Such wishes may be made before a Buddha image or any other object which represents noble ideals and virtues, such as a Bodhi tree (a symbol of enlightenment), a shrine, a pagoda, etc. Such wishes are not mere wishful thinking or idle prayers, but positive resolutions for wholesome actions. They are necessary for the accomplishment of certain desired goals and are referred to in Pali as *adhiṭṭhāna*. *Adhiṭṭhāna*, in fact, constitutes one of the ten Perfections that are a prerequisite for the realization of *Nibbāna*. Thus, a person may make a wish before a Buddha image saying, "May I have the strength to help others in need. May I have the opportunity to do more good every day." Or an aspirant to enlightenment may make determined wishes before a Buddha to attain Buddhahood in some future life. Certainly, there is a great difference between such wishes and someone saying before a Buddha image, "O Lord, may I obtain a beautiful, young wife" or "May I become a millionaire tomorrow!"

# 4

# THE DHAMMA

## THE MEANING OF DHAMMA

ETYMOLOGICALLY, THE WORD DHAMMA (Sanskrit: *Dharma*) is derived from the root "dhar," meaning "to uphold" or "to support," and the commentary further explains that it is that which upholds or supports the practitioner (of Dhamma) and prevents him or her from falling into evil states or birth in a woeful existence.

Of all Buddhist terminology, the word Dhamma commands the widest and most comprehensive meaning. There is nothing that does not come within the purview of this word. In fact, all things, animate or inanimate, all phenomena, those that can be seen or felt and those beyond our empirical perception, all conditioned and unconditioned states, can be included in the term Dhamma. However, Dhamma as one of the Three Gems is represented by the teachings of the Buddha.

The late Venerable Buddhadāsa, one of the most influential thinkers and Dhamma exponents in contemporary Thailand, explains the meaning of the term by a fourfold definition. According to this, Dhamma means (a) the state of nature as it is, (b) the laws of nature, (c) the duties that must be performed in accordance with the laws of nature, and (d) the results that are derived from the fulfillment of such duties. This definition, he claims, represents the true and complete picture of Dhamma, and is inclusive of all things which the term refers to.

Buddhadāsa's explanation closely follows the pattern of the Four Noble Truths, found in the very first discourse of the Buddha. The first Truth deals with *dukkha* (suffering), a Pali term which characterizes all things that exist. *Dukkha* represents the state of nature as it is, which is the first of the four definitions of Dhamma. The second Truth deals with the cause of *dukkha*, comparable with the laws of nature, for it is on the laws of nature that things (*dukkha*) arise, function, and cease. The third Truth deals with the extinction of *dukkha*, a state of complete freedom experienced as a result (fourth definition) of the efforts to fulfill the duty of Dhamma. The fourth Truth deals with the path leading to the cessation of *dukkha*, which is comparable to the third definition of Dhamma (duty to be fulfilled according to the laws of nature). By treading the path of Dhamma (performing duties) one obtains results proportionate to one's endeavor—being free from *dukkha*.

Understanding the Dhamma in its broadest sense, according to the doctrine of the four Noble Truths, helps us to see how closely it is related to our lives and how we can perceive all aspects of our lives and activities in the light of the Dhamma. For example, we can clearly see Dhamma in our experience of hunger, something very common in life. Hunger is part of nature, a natural state of existence, which we feel the way it is (*dukkha*). It arises, according to the laws of nature, from certain conditions—namely, lack of food. Nature further dictates that we must perform appropriate duties with regard to hunger, that is, we take necessary actions according to the laws of nature (fourth Noble Truth) by eating. As a result, hunger is appeased and we experience freedom from its pains (third Noble Truth).

Of course, this is simply an analogy of how an ordinary experience may be perceived from the perspective of the Dhamma. It does not specifically mean that eating constitutes the fourth Noble Truth, nor is the extinction of physical hunger really the third Truth as intended by the Buddha. The analogy demonstrates the practical purpose that understanding the Dhamma in relation to our direct experiences, and in the light of the Four Noble Truths, serves, especially since such an attitude enables us to live constantly in the presence of the Dhamma itself. The fourfold definition of Dhamma points to the infinite scope of the term as well as the inseparability of life and Dhamma.

## ATTRIBUTES OF THE DHAMMA

There are six qualities attributed to the Dhamma in the Pali scriptures. These virtuous qualities are described in the meditation technique known as Recollection of the Dhamma (*dhammānussati*). Understanding these attributes also helps to increase conviction and faith in the Dhamma.

The first attribute of the Dhamma is its comprehensive exposition by the Buddha, who realized it through his direct experience. The Buddha's omniscience and boundless compassion assure us of the validity and value of his teachings, which are "fine in the beginning, fine in the middle, and fine in the end, complete with meanings and principles for living a noble life leading to purity and complete freedom."

Secondly, the Dhamma is realizable through its practitioners' own efforts. Those who practice the Buddha's teachings will see the Dhamma for themselves. They will derive the full benefits of their own commitment and will thereby be convinced of the truth of the Dhamma. Thus, there is no need to blindly believe in what is said by others.

The third attribute of Dhamma is expressed in the Pali term *akālika*, which is translated either as "timeless" or "yielding immediate results." The Dhamma is timeless because it transcends all temporal limitations; its truth is eternal. The Dhamma is said to yield immediate results because its effects can be experienced at each and every moment. The principle of conditionality, for instance, demonstrates how each phenomenon is a conditioned and conditioning link in a continuous flux of ever-changing events. Buddhist commentators also explain *akālika* as the immediate attainment of results represented by the fruition consciousness (*phalacitta*) that successively follows the path consciousness (*maggacitta*) in the psychological process of transcendent realization. But this explanation is rather technical. In fact, the commentators specifically assign all attributes of the Dhamma, except the first, to transcendent experiences (*lokuttaradhamma*), although they can be more conveniently understood in the light of mundane perception.

The fourth attribute of the Dhamma is *ehipassika*, usually rendered into English as "come and see." This really means that the Dhamma is completely open to investigation and verification. Because Dhamma is Truth, its worth and value do not depend on belief or faith, but are open to thorough examination and reexamination by all Truth seekers. The Buddha himself strongly advised his disciples not to blindly believe in him, but to question and re-question until they were fully convinced of the teacher and the teachings (the Dhamma). He further encouraged them to put the Dhamma to test by practising it, "just as a goldsmith tests the purity of his gold by cutting, rubbing, and burning it."

Next, the Dhamma is said to lead to higher knowledge and the realization of *Nibbāna*. This quality makes the practice of Dhamma highly rewarding, for the ultimate realization (of Dhamma) means the highest bliss and complete freedom from all suffering.

The sixth attribute of the Dhamma is an often quoted one. The Pali term for it is *paccattaṁ*, which means that the Dhamma as an experience is directly known through intuitive insight and is thus a matter of personal knowledge. It is true that it can be heard from others, but to really know the Dhamma, such secondhand knowledge is insufficient. A direct experience is the most crucial factor in the realization of the Truth.

Direct experience is especially important where *Nibbāna* is concerned. In our normal day-to-day activities, even in the most ordinary matters, doubt and uncertainty arise from time to time when we lack direct experience of the things we have to deal with. Emotional sentiments also require personal experience to really understand, they cannot be understood through logic or verbal explanation. With personal experience, doubt and uncertainty disappear. The Dhamma is a matter of personal experience. *Paccattaṁ* implies wisdom or the ability to understand things deeply and correctly, according to their true nature. Without a base of direct experience, doubt and uncertainty regarding the Dhamma can still arise. But with *paccattaṁ*, or self-realization, there is no room for such doubts.

## THE PRESERVATION OF THE BUDDHA'S TEACHINGS

The Buddha gave spontaneous discourses, attuned to particular listeners and situations. Originally, these discourses were collectively referred to as Dhamma-Vinaya, or the Doctrine and Discipline. They were memorized and preserved orally by the *bhikkhus*, who consequently specialized in reciting certain sections of the discourses. For example, Venerable Ānanda, the Buddha's personal attendant for many years, was well-versed in the doctrine (Dhamma), while Venerable Upāli, another prominent disciple, was preeminent in the discipline (Vinaya). The Buddha's teachings were preserved in this manner from one generation of monks to another until they were committed into writing in Sri Lanka some 500 years after the Buddha's *Parinibbāna*.

After the Buddha passed away, councils were held from time to time to discuss important issues and pressing problems that had arisen within the Saṅgha. At such councils, the Dhamma-Vinaya was recited to ensure its purity and authenticity. Finally, the teachings were grouped together under three categories, collectively known as *Tipiṭaka* or the Three Baskets.

The first is the *Vinaya Piṭaka*, the 'basket' of Discipline, which deals with rules and regulations laid down by the Buddha for monastic members. The second is the *Sutta* (or *Suttanta*) *Piṭaka*, the 'basket' of Discourses, which contains the Buddha's many sermons or expositions of the Dhamma given to a wide range of listeners on various occasions. The third is the *Abhidhamma Piṭaka*, the 'basket' of Higher Dhamma, which by and large discusses at great length the philosophical and psychological aspects of the Buddha's teachings.

The *Tipiṭaka* is the most sacred literature of Buddhists, believed to contain the words of the Buddha as preserved through the ages by his monk disciples. It is indeed a colossal work, containing as many as 24.23 million characters in Thai script (many more if written in Roman script). Together with the earlier commentaries written by his disciples, not to mention the later ones, the whole collection of Buddhist classical literature contains more than 61.4 million characters in Thai script. The *Tipiṭaka* has been translated into many languages, and is widely read. A good part of the earlier commentaries have also been translated from the Pali originals, some of which, like Venerable Buddhaghosa's Path of Purification (*Visuddhimagga*), are quite widely circulated and enjoy great popularity.

## LAY STUDY OF THE TIPIṬAKA

Although the *Tipiṭaka* and its commentaries are a vast storehouse of religious knowledge and spiritual experience, a layman need not despair of mastering the subject. While it is true that a detailed study of the *Tipiṭaka* and other sacred texts is a profound and time-consuming endeavor best left to specialists or monks, since birth as a Buddhist and having access to the Dhamma is a rare privilege, no responsible Buddhist should neglect this opportunity to get acquainted with the Buddha's teachings. Despite family obligations and worldly concerns, lay Buddhists should endeavor to study the Dhamma as much as they can, concentrating on those discourses that appeal to them and are relevant to their needs. At the very least, some basic understanding of the religion and how to practise it in daily life can be gained. It is within everyone's capacity to accomplish this, and such efforts will be immensely rewarding, not only from the spiritual point of view, but from the perspective of material success as well.

The five precepts, for example, are fundamental to all Buddhists, offering a practical guideline for moral conduct. Then there are the four Noble Truths, the four Virtues of Householders, the six Directions of a Householder's Obligations, the six Downfalls, the seven Virtues of a Lay Buddhist, and numerous other teachings, which are quite accessible to ordinary people and give clear indications of how a good and useful life can be led. Following the path of Dhamma leads to happiness and freedom from the problems commonly associated with an immoral life.

Buddhism is a religion of wisdom, and Buddhists should be wise enough to perceive the value of the teaching and make a sincere effort to understand their religion. With Buddhism widely available and access to Buddhist teachers and literature relatively easy today, there is no excuse for Buddhists not becoming better informed in the Dhamma.

## THE DHAMMA AS REFUGE

A refuge provides shelter from danger. Naturally, this is something that all beings need. Even wild animals need some form of protection or other, such as forests or caves. Some people seek protection in wealth, believing that it can help solve their problems; some seek protection from powerful people. There are also those who worship deities in order to seek their protection and favor. Taking refuge (in the broadest sense of the term) is therefore almost instinctual, a matter of survival for all sentient beings. Human beings take refuge, seeking fulfillment of their material or emotional needs, in accordance with their beliefs, consciously or otherwise. Some refuges are sublime, some are gross, and others are just products of the imagination.

The Dhamma is a refuge *par excellence*. It provides true and lasting protection, not false hope or temporary shelter. It provides happiness and security not only in this life but the next, and even enables the attainment of the highest bliss of *Nibbāna*. But it is necessary to learn the proper way to take refuge in the Dhamma, and understand how the Dhamma can be a true refuge. This may be better understood through an analogy:

A good medicine is useful to a patient only when it is taken properly. Even the best cure will be as useless as any other concoction if this fact is not taken into account. Likewise, the Dhamma can only be of true benefit when it is practised properly. The Buddha has been compared to a great physician, one who clearly diagnosed the spiritual ills of humanity and prescribed the Dhamma as a remedy. Recognizing this fact, it is our duty to follow that prescription and try earnestly to practise the Dhamma. Only then can the Dhamma really become our refuge. Thus, even if the Buddha and the Dhamma are there, ultimately it is each and every one of us who must make the effort, just as much as it rests with the patient to seek treatment and take medicine for himself, notwithstanding the availability of the best physician and the most efficacious medicine. There is a saying in *Jātaka Nipāta* which is worth considering in this matter:

"If a sick man seeks not treatment even when a physician is at hand, the physician is not to blame. In the same way, if a man is afflicted with the disease of defilements but seeks not the help of the Buddha (does not practise Dhamma), then the Buddha is not to blame."

Just as there are different types of medicines to suit different ailments, so are the Buddha's discourses and the virtues to be cultivated according to his teachings many and varied. Improper use of the Dhamma, based on ignorance or wrong view, may not produce the desired results, so it is important to understand it correctly. For instance, hatred and anger should be countered by love and kindness; excessive attachment to sensual pleasures should be checked by constant reflection on the impermanent nature of things; greed and selfishness should be countered with generosity and service to others; mental restlessness should be corrected by the practice of concentration meditation; compassion should be cultivated along side with wisdom, etc. In this way the Dhamma can be a true refuge.

To be protected by the Dhamma it is, therefore, essential to take the initiative in the practice of the Dhamma. We must be open and receptive to the Dhamma. If we are willing to practise the Dhamma in daily life by refraining, for instance, from evil or unskillful actions, it is not difficult to see how the Dhamma will protect us from problems and undesirable experiences and will help us to attain happiness and progress in life.

## IS BUDDHISM A PHILOSOPHY OR AN ETHICAL SYSTEM?

Terms like philosophy and ethics are used to designate certain disciplines of human thought and behavior. These usually result from logic and speculative thinking, but the Dhamma is the Truth discovered by the Buddha as a result of his supreme enlightenment. The Dhamma is a way of life, a system of thought by which we live and on which we base our moral conduct. Both philosophy and ethics can be found embodied in the Dhamma, but the Dhamma covers a much wider scope.

When the Buddha taught the Dhamma, he did not intend it to be characterized as either philosophy or ethics, he simply explained the Truth and the course of action to follow in order to lead a happy and useful life. For example, the first discourse, given to a group of five ascetics, begins with his warning against the two courses of practice that were in vogue at that time, but which he considered to be useless, ignoble, and unprofitable. These are the extremes of indulgence in sensual gratification and the practice of self-mortification. Then he explained the Four Noble Truths, which represent the reality of existence in all its aspects. Finally, he taught the Noble Eightfold Path, which is the course of practice to realize the Dhamma. At the end of the discourse, one of the ascetics is said to have attained to the higher knowledge known as the Eye of Truth (*dhammacakkhu*).

On another occasion, when the Blessed One saw a young man at a crossroads worshipping and prostrating in different directions, he advised him that a nobler and better method of worship was to properly perform one's duties toward other members of society. The Buddha compared social relationships to the different directions which the young man had been worshipping. According to the Buddha, the best way to worship them is by fulfilling one's duties in the light of those relationships. Fulfilling one's duties is, in fact, the highest form of worship.

The Buddha mentioned six kinds of relationship, which he compared to the six directions. Accordingly, parents are compared to the eastern direction, teachers are likened to the southern direction, spouse and children to the west, friends to the north, servants and employees to the nadir, and monks to the zenith. To each of these people there are certain duties to fulfill, and fulfilling them is by far a nobler kind of worship. The Buddha also explained in detail the different duties that are inherent in these six kinds of social relationships, beginning with how parents should care for their children, and how the children should reciprocate their parents' love and kindness, and so on and so forth.

It is true that certain discourses or teachings of the Dhamma may be deemed to come within the scope of either philosophy or ethics and may be designated as such. However, one needs to keep in mind that as far as the Dhamma is concerned, such designations are immaterial and add nothing of value to the Buddha's teachings.

## THE UNIVERSALITY OF THE DHAMMA

Universality and timelessness are two most distinct characteristics of the Dhamma. These two characteristics are based on the fact that the Dhamma is Truth itself, not a set of theories or principles. It is therefore not subject to any spatial or temporal limitations, like laws or conventions which are products of human invention.

If something is created, or claimed to have been created, the foundation of such creation remains on shifting ground, and will therefore be subject to spatiotemporal restrictions. The laws of one country, for instance, will become irrelevant in another (spatial restriction); or what has been deemed appropriate at a certain point of time will become inapplicable at another (temporal restriction). The same thing can be said of cultures, traditions, or conventions, which are all human creations. Even religious beliefs claimed to have been connected with God fall into this category and are not free from the same weaknesses. They may serve certain purposes for some groups of people or for some periods of time, but they lack the two important characteristics of universality and timelessness, even if efforts have been made to claim them.

The Dhamma, on the other hand, is not created. When the Buddha proclaimed the Dhamma, he did not invent it. What he did was simply proclaim the Truth, which he had realized through his own efforts and wisdom. He did not imagine things, nor did he find it necessary to claim God's grace in order to win followers. His teachings represent the Truth, which is universal and timeless.

The Buddhist doctrine of conditionality states, for example, that all things and phenomena are conditioned and interrelated; there is nothing that is not conditioned or is absolute in itself. This is a simple statement of the Truth. Based on this are the law of cause and effect, the law of *kamma,* and the law of dependent origination, which are all different manifestations of the same Truth and which are, likewise, universal and timeless. Even when the Buddha taught that all things are impermanent and are subject to change, he was simply revealing the eternal Truth of existence, not his own imagination or assumptions. On one occasion he said: "Whatever is of the nature to arise, that very thing is of the nature to disappear." This is sometimes referred to as the law of change, and it can easily be seen how this truth will remain forever valid, irrespective of time and place. Such is the nature and quality of the Buddha's teachings.

Universality implies three fundamental characteristics: 1) the inclusion of all things and phenomena, collectively or individually; 2) an all-embracing nature that transcends limits without exception; and 3) being in existence or operation everywhere and under all conditions. Thus, the universality of Dhamma means that all people, animals, deities, and things, without exception, exist in the Dhamma and that the Dhamma exists and operates in all of those phenomena. This is the omnipresent quality of the Dhamma, and it is important to understand this clearly in order to be convinced of our unity with the Dhamma.

The timelessness of the Dhamma is also characterized by three attributes: First, it implies an eternal state of being without beginning and end. If something is created, it must necessarily have a beginning; and beginning consequently points to the other extreme, which is the end of things so created. Whatever is subject to creation is, therefore, never eternal. Secondly, timelessness means freedom from restriction in time. Thirdly, timelessness denotes the fact that the Dhamma can be proved in its validity and consistency under all temporal conditions, according to its own laws.

As the third attribute of the Dhamma, timelessness is expressed by the Pali term *akālika*, which is rendered into English either as "timeless" or "yielding immediate results." As has been pointed out, the Dhamma is eternal, beyond temporal conditions. It is interpreted as yielding immediate results to demonstrate how it can be continually experienced from moment to moment. Commentators construe timelessness to mean the subsequent attainment of resultant consciousness as occurring in the mental process of transcendent realization and represented by one of the four *phalacitta* (fruition consciousness) that immediately follows the corresponding *maggacitta* (path consciousness).

The Dhamma is therefore not bounded by space-time factors; it is practical and applicable to all places and times, although it requires understanding and wisdom to put its principles into practice and applied to real life situations.

## ALLOWANCE FOR CHANGE

Before passing away, the Buddha authorized the Saṅgha to abrogate "minor and lesser" disciplinary rules that they might consider inapplicable or irrelevant in later times. He did not allow them to change or modify the Dhamma. This is another good example of the axiom that whatever is created is always subject to space-time considerations and, therefore, lacks the characteristics of universality and timelessness. Because the Vinaya rules were formulated by the Buddha, he foresaw the need to rescind or modify some of them in accordance with changing circumstances and later developments. That is why he made his position clear to the assembly of disciples who were present at the Great Demise. However, the Saṅgha made a collective decision at the First Council to preserve them and try to keep them intact, out of their love and respect for the Buddha, in order to prevent future indiscretions by individuals who might attempt to take advantage of the Buddha's permission.

The Dhamma, on the other hand, was not something that the Buddha had formulated for his disciples. It was revealed and proclaimed according to the Truth he had discovered. Thus it requires neither abrogation nor modification to suit later opinions or philosophical developments.

## THE ESSENCE OF DHAMMA

The Buddha declared the doctrine of Dependent Origination (*Paṭiccasamuppāda*) to be a very profound and difficult subject. Its profundity and difficulty rest on both its theory and practice. In fact, soon after his enlightenment the Buddha spent a whole week meditating on this particular Dhamma. This doctrine is one of the subjects the Buddha often taught to his monks. Once Venerable Ānanda casually remarked that it seemed easy to understand, but the Buddha hastened to correct him with a clear warning :

> "Say not so, Ānanda, say not so! The doctrine of Dependent Origination is profound, difficult to understand. Sentient beings, through not understanding this doctrine proclaimed by me, are befuddled like a tangled and knotted ball of twine, or like a disorderly heap of tangled threads, or an untended thicket of weeds, or like entangled reeds. In such wise are those sentient beings ensnared, unable to liberate themselves from *Saṁsāra*, from suffering, and from the states of hell and downfall."

The doctrine of Dependent Origination was specifically recommended by the Buddha for monks to study. It is one of the doctrines about which the Buddha had admonished his followers not to be divided or contentious, and which he asserted would be "for the great benefit of mankind, for the well-being of the world, and for the advantage of gods and humans."

The doctrine of Dependent Origination helps to clarify the Buddhist position concerning the false view of a permanent self (*attā*). According to the teaching, nothing is absolute, nothing is permanent, for all things arise, exist, and cease depending on causes and conditions. Since all things are conditioned, interdependent, and interrelated, the existence of a permanent self is a logical impossibility.

The principle underlying the doctrine of Dependent Origination has been succinctly summarized by the Buddha in a formula of four sentences:

This is, that is (*imasmiṁ sati idaṁ hoti*);
This arising, that arises (*imassuppāda idaṁ uppajjati*);
This is not, that is not (*imasmiṁ asati idaṁ na hoti*);
This ceasing, that ceases (*imassa nirodha idaṁ nirujjhati*).

This short formula covers the whole scope of existence and clearly demonstrates the interrelationship of all things. Based on this principle of conditionality and interdependence, the doctrine of Dependent Origination is explained in many different forms. However, the best-known mode of exposition consists in the circle of twelve links that are connected together by the law of conditionality :

1. Dependent on delusion are *kamma*-formations.
2. Dependent on *kamma*-formations is consciousness.
3. Dependent on consciousness are mental and physical phenomena.
4. Dependent on mental and physical phenomena are the six faculties of physical sense-bases and mind.
5. Dependent on the six faculties is (sensorial and mental) contact.
6. Dependent on contact is feeling.
7. Dependent on feeling is craving (desire).
8. Dependent on craving is attachment (clinging).
9. Dependent on attachment is becoming.

10. Dependent on becoming is birth.

11. Dependent on birth are (12) decay, death, sorrow, lamentation, pain, grief, and despair.

The doctrine of Dependent Origination also clearly invalidates the concept of a first cause. Each of the twelve links serves both as a conditioning as well as a conditioned factor. When all things are interconnected and interdependent, as shown by the law of conditionality, the idea of a first cause naturally becomes irrelevant. Following along the same line of exposition, the Buddha also points out how the whole structure ceases to be. Thus, dependent on the cessation of delusion, kamma-formations cease; dependent on the cessation of kamma-formations, consciousness ceases; dependent on the cessation of consciousness, mental and physical phenomena cease, etc.

The practical objective of the doctrine of Dependent Origination is to show how suffering (*dukkha*) arises and how it can be brought to an end. Likewise, by having a correct understanding of this teaching, we come to perceive how *Saṁsāra* arises and continues, and most importantly, how it can be ended. *Nibbāna* is attained through the cessation of *Saṁsāra*. Having thoroughly penetrated the doctrine of Dependent Origination, one learns how to completely unravel the knot of suffering and become a true master of oneself. In this way, one becomes truly free and liberated.

The Buddha explained the Dhamma in many different ways to best suit his audience's intellectual and spiritual maturity, but his teachings all point to the same Truth and lead to the same goal.

In one of the verses in the Dhammapada, the Buddha has said: "Not to do evil; to do good; and to purify the mind, this is the teaching of all Buddhas." This statement is often cited as the heart of Buddhist practice. To follow the path of the Buddha is, therefore, the giving up of what is morally unwholesome, the doing of which brings about undesirable consequences. Observance of moral precepts laid down by the Buddha is one way to put this principle into practice. In addition, one learns to do good by performing wholesome actions, such as charity, social services, supporting one's parents, cultivation of kindness and compassion, and so on. These two basic principles are of great value and add to individual as well as social growth. But the spiritual effort needs to go one step further. By purifying the mind, one moves up on the ladder of spiritual advancement and experiences bliss and happiness on a higher level that is not readily accessible to non-practitioners. Purification of the mind is achieved through meditation practice, which is praised by the Buddha as one of the most direct ways to enlightenment. So these three principles can be said to constitute the Buddhist modes of ethical practice, and we have it from the Buddha himself that they also constitute the teachings of all Buddhas.

Elsewhere the Buddha proclaimed: "I teach nothing but *dukkha* (unsatisfactoriness) and the extinction of *dukkha*." This statement is, of course, made in the context of the Four Noble Truths, considered by most scholars to be the central teaching of Buddhist philosophy. This is another example of how the one Dhamma can be expressed in different ways. Those who understand the essence of the Dhamma will see the unity of all the different doctrinal themes and how they are fundamentally interrelated.

An integral part of the Four Noble Truths is the Noble Eightfold Path, which comprises right view, right thought, right speech, right action, right livelihood, right effort, right mindfulness, and right concentration. The three principles of abstention from evil, doing what is good, and purification of mind can all fit into the framework of the Noble Eightfold Path. We may even assert that they are the same things expressed differently. In fact, like the threefold training of morality, concentration and wisdom, they are the Noble Eightfold Path expressed in another way. Thus we can see the characteristic unity and coherence in all of the Buddha's teachings.

# MIND PURIFICATION

As a religion, Buddhism gives much importance to the cultivation of mind and mental faculties. Life consists of two closely interconnected components, the body and the mind, which constantly demand our care and attention. Of these two, mind is said to be of paramount importance for it is the very source of all actions that we do from birth to death. We are what we think. Therefore, it is crucial that we have the right understanding of our minds and know how to train them properly.

Mind is not as concrete and objective as the body, and most people give only little concern to their minds, taking more interest in their physical forms and appearances. The body is well-nourished, kept clean, and beautified, while the mind is almost totally neglected. The Dhamma is nourishment for the mind; it cleanses the mind, and makes the mind pleasant and beautiful. Just as an undernourished body is weak and becomes a seat of disease, a mind starved of Dhamma is also weak and becomes a source of problems. Crime, corruption, violence, and immoral behavior are some of the symptoms of a mind which is uncared for, uncleansed, and unbeautified by the Dhamma. It is therefore important to train the mind, and the best way to do this is through meditation.

Mental purification is not an end in itself, neither is it an activity separate from real life situations. To practise meditation by no means necessitates giving up family, leaving home, and retiring to a forest or a cave, although such would be ideal for a monk. The process of mental purification itself necessarily involves a morally skillful life-style and the practice of the other two principles of abstention from evil and doing wholesome deeds. Thus it can be seen that this more refined practice has a direct bearing on both individual and social well-being and is a truly beneficial commitment. Moreover, an action which springs from a pure mind will naturally be free from evil and full of wholesome qualities. A pure mind, indeed, is a natural and unlimited source of good actions and benevolent deeds. Says the Buddha: "Mind is the forerunner of all mental states, mind is their chief, they are all mind-made. If one speaks or acts with a pure mind, then happiness follows one as a shadow its owner."

Thus, mental purification is not practised solely for its own sake, but for individual as well as social benefit. Its impact on personal behavior and society can be truly tremendous.

## THE PROFUNDITY OF THE DHAMMA

Soon after the Buddha's enlightenment, as he was contemplating the Dhamma, its sheer profundity became clear to him. He was assailed by doubt over whether it would not be futile to expound the Dhamma to the world, enveloped as it is in the veil of ignorance and overcome by greed and hatred. The Dhamma, reflected the Buddha, goes against the flow of worldly thoughts and is difficult for people to accept. But out of wisdom and compassion, he also perceived the different levels of people's intellectual and spiritual maturity. Those "with less dust in their eyes," having less delusion and defilements, would listen and understand, they would benefit from the Dhamma. Thus the Buddha decided to begin the mission that eventually led to the establishment of the Buddhist religion.

Although the Dhamma is profound, it is not inaccessible. The fact that there have been so many Arahants and noble disciples, thousands upon thousands of them, both during and after the Buddha's time, stands as a testimony to the intelligibility and practicality of the Dhamma. Through his skillful means, the Buddha placed the task of understanding the Dhamma within reach of every interested person.

Moreover, the Buddha has provided us with an amazing variety of teachings to choose from. Not only is there teaching for those intent on achieving the ultimate realization of *Nibbāna*, but there is more than enough teaching for those who are content to remain involved in the ordinary business of mundane affairs. An opportunity is never denied those who care to seek. If only we pay attention, we will see the Dhamma in everything around us and in all existential realities. Even children are capable of understanding the Dhamma, as very well demonstrated by the fact that during the time of the Buddha quite a few children, as young as seven years of age, are reported to have attained Arahantship. Certainly, the profundity of the Dhamma is no excuse for denying yourself that which is best in life.

Many Buddhists see practising the Dhamma as an act of merit making. Merits are accumulated, for instance, by a charitable act, by observing precepts, or by practising meditation. Becoming an Arahant in the present life is never seen as a goal for such people. Although such an attitude may not be considered the most ideal, yet such people are following the path of Dhamma at their own pace. There is no reason why the path should not be followed by those who wish to continue to practice as householders. On more than one occasion, the Buddha eloquently praised his householder disciples, who were diligently practising the Dhamma by engaging in various meritorious activities. This should also be an inspiration to those who find the Buddhist philosophy and the Dhamma practice on a higher level somewhat daunting.

# 5

# THE SANGHA

## THE MEANING AND SIGNIFICANCE OF SANGHA

THE SANGHA FORMS THE THIRD COMPONENT of the Triple Gem. Sangha members represent the embodiment of the Dhamma and they have been, by and large, responsible for the preservation and promotion of the religion, both during and after the time of the Buddha.

Two months after his enlightenment the Buddha began his teaching mission by delivering the first sermon, called the *Dhammacakkappavattana Sutta,* to a group of five ascetics, who were his former associates. They were Kondañña, Vappa, Bhaddiya, Mahānāma, and Assaji. At the conclusion of the discourse, Kondañña is said to have attained the "Eye of Truth," i.e., realized the Dhamma and achieved the first of four stages of transcendent spiritual attainment. With that, the Sangha came into being, bringing to completion the Holy Triple Gem. This happened on the full moon day of the month *Āsāḷha* (eighth lunar month).

Literally, Sangha means community. In its broadest sense, the term covers both the lay and the monastic communities. From the doctrinal perspective, it refers to those who have achieved any of the four stages of transcendent spiritual attainment. Such Saṅgha members are known as 'noble disciples' (*ariyasaṅgha*). Technically, these are called *Sotāpanna* (Stream Enterer), *Sakadāgāmi* (Once Returner), *Anāgāmi* (Non-Returner), and *Arahanta* (Worthy One). These noble disciples constitute the Saṅgha of the Triple Gem; they are Saṅgha by virtue of their special attainments. Thus anyone who has attained to that higher level is qualified to be included in this category of Saṅgha.

From the perspective of the Vinaya (Discipline), Saṅgha refers to a community of monks (*bhikkhusaṅgha*), specifically a group of four or more monks, who are required to be present at certain ecclesiastical rites where a quorum of monastic members is needed. This is the Saṅgha according to the Vinaya definition, but not necessarily as part of the Triple Gem. Thus there are two categories of Saṅgha, namely, Noble Saṅgha and Conventional Saṅgha. Of course, individual monks may belong to both if they are so qualified. Kondañña and his colleagues, and many of their contemporaries, were some of these noble monk disciples.

However, because the role of the monks is so distinct and prominent, the term Saṅgha is often used exclusively in reference to the community of monks and does not cover the laity as in its broader sense. In the Theravada tradition, especially, this term is never used in connection with the lay community.

When Kondañña gained the Eye of Truth, he became the first member of the Noble Saṅgha. When he was ordained a monk, he became the first member of the Conventional Saṅgha. Thus, the conclusion of the first discourse marks the beginning of the Noble as well as the Conventional Saṅgha of disciples.

## THE POSITION OF SAṄGHA IN THE TRIPLE GEM

By realizing the Dhamma, members of the Saṅgha most effectively vindicate the Buddha's claim of enlightenment, thereby bringing

his supreme achievement to full fruition. The Buddha's enlightenment was, no doubt, the fruit of a long and difficult process, but it
was meant for a much broader purpose than his own exclusive
benefit; his effort was based on universal compassion and inspired
by the selfless desire to serve mankind. If there was no one to
understand the Dhamma after him, his enlightenment would be
of no use to others. Thus the Saṅgha was instrumental in enabling
Buddhahood to accomplish its full purpose and fruition. In this
way, the Buddha achieved both his own benefit as well as benefit
for the world.

Members of the Saṅgha were indispensable in the spread and
preservation of the Buddha's message, both during his lifetime and
long after his death, down to the present time. They act as the
principal guardians of the faith. Without the Saṅgha the religion
could not endure and prosper. This is evident from the fact that
even in the areas where Buddhism was introduced earlier, if the
Saṅgha were not well established, the religion would soon die out.
Thanks to the Saṅgha, the world now has relatively convenient
access to the Buddha's teachings and can still enjoy the fruit of the
Buddha's enlightenment.

The Saṅgha demonstrates to us that it is possible to realize the
Dhamma and become enlightened. Their examples are a vivid and
important source of moral support to all of us who are not yet well
established in the path of spiritual practice. In time of doubt and
uncertainty, we can always turn to them for advice and instruction. If the Buddha's teachings appear too idealistic, we have
assurance and encouragement in the Saṅgha, who show us that it
is humanly possible to lead such an ideal life and to realize the
highest religious goal.

## THE ATTRIBUTES OF THE NOBLE SAṄGHA

In Buddhist meditation there is a method of practice in which meditators learn to contemplate on the virtues of the Saṅgha (*Saṅghānussati*). In addition, the Buddhist system of worship includes a recitation of the Saṅgha's virtues as a means of reflection and as a concentration exercise. Nine attributes of the Saṅgha are enumerated. The Saṅgha is said to be of good conduct, of upright conduct, of wise conduct, of seemly conduct; the Saṅgha is worthy of gifts, worthy of hospitality, worthy of offerings, worthy of reverential salutation; the Saṅgha is the incomparable field of merits to the world.

Attaining one of the four stages of transcendent spirituality is a prerequisite for qualification as a member of the Noble Saṅgha. In fact, these four stages can be attained only in successive order starting from the first. It therefore follows that once an individual achieves the first stage, he becomes, immediately and permanently, a member of the Noble Saṅgha by the very virtue of that achievement. It is this very first stage that the expression Eye of Truth refers to. Subsequent attainment of the more exalted stages hardly affects one's status as a member of the Noble Saṅgha, although it does mean higher development and greater progress in spiritual advancement.

## THE FOUR LEVELS OF NOBLE SAṄGHA

The four levels of transcendent attainment may be described as follows:

1.) *Sotāpanna*. This literally means Stream Entry, a metaphorical expression suggesting a stage where one 'enters' into the stream of *Nibbāna*. It is a spiritual sphere beyond the mundane and is therefore not liable to relapse. Once this stage is attained, the noble disciple will be inexorably swept toward the ultimate attainment of Arahantship and nothing can stand in his way. He will not be reborn more than seven times at the most before attaining Arahantship, neither will he ever be born in any woeful states (below that of human).

A Stream-Enterer is incapable of breaking the five precepts because he has permanently eliminated the lowest 'fetters' from his mind. There are ten kinds of defilements called fetters (saṁyojana) that bind worldlings to Saṁsāra or the cycle of birth and death. Out of these ten, a Stream-Enterer has destroyed the first three, doing away with the false view of individuality (sakkāyadiṭṭhi), doubt in the Triple Gem, in the doctrine of kamma, and the four Noble Truths (vicikicchā), and blind attachment to rites and rituals (sīlabbataparāmāsa). These are three of the five lower fetters that are abandoned on the attainment of Stream-Entry.

There are three classes of Stream-Enterers: those who, if not attaining to arahantship in this very life, will be born only once before attaining Arahantship; those who will take only two or three births before the final deliverance; and those who will be born seven more times at the most before the ultimate realization of Nibbāna. Characteristic of Stream-Enterers is their perfect moral integrity, not given to committing even a relatively insignificant immoral act, even though they may still lead the life of householders. They have complete and unshakable faith in the Triple Gem and would neither denounce nor renounce it at any cost.

2.) Sakadāgāmi. This is a further refinement from Stream-Entry. Literally, the term means Once-Returner, referring to the fact that a noble disciple who has attained this stage is subject to only one more birth before attaining Arahantship. This means that a Once-Returner will attain the final liberation in the very next life if not in the present.

In addition to the three Fetters destroyed in the first stage of Stream-Entry, the Once-Returner further mitigates the three roots of defilements, namely, greed, anger, and delusion. At this stage one has become so advanced in spiritual development that one is almost completely free from the grosser impurities (kilesa).

3.) *Anāgāmi*. The term is usually translated as Non-Returner. This is an even higher stage of spiritual development, which the noble disciple attains on eliminating the remaining two of the five Lower Fetters (the first three have been destroyed at the attainment of Stream-Entry). These two are lust or attachment to sensual pleasure (*kāmarāga*) and the defilement of aversion (*paṭigha*), which causes anger, irritation, ill will, and so on.

As a rule, because lust and greed have been removed, a Non-Returner is not inclined to remain a householder (if he is one). He is likely to take to the life of renunciation by entering the monastic Order, for instance, or becoming a recluse. With the destruction of lust and anger, he is not bound to birth in any of the lower planes of existence. After death, Non-Returners are reborn only in one of the five Abodes of the Pure (*suddhāvāsa*), where no beings other than a Non-Returner are born, and from where they finally attain *Nibbāna*.

4.) *Arahanta* (normally spelt Arahant). This is the highest stage of spiritual attainment, which a noble disciple reaches through the complete eradication of all defilements, including the five higher fetters, which are attachment to the realms of form (*rūparāga*), attachment to immaterial or formless planes of existence (*arūparāga*), conceit (*māna*), restlessness (*uddhacca*), and ignorance or delusion (*avijjā*). An Arahant, or Worthy One, is said to have accomplished what needs to be accomplished: being perfect, the Arahant has no further need to practise for his own sake. Although continuing to serve fellow beings, teaching and giving them advice, the Arahant accumulates no fresh *kamma*, working not for his or her own good but solely for the good of others. Being free from all kinds of defilements, the arahant lives in perfect calm and equanimity, not given to such negative emotions as lust, greed, jealousy, anger, and aggression. The Arahant becomes one with the Buddha in purity of heart, in wisdom and compassion. This is the ultimate achievement, the highest spiritual development any individual may strive for. It is the same state which the

Buddha attained in his enlightenment.

The Worthy One transcends the conditions of birth and death. At the final moment of his present life, he is said to pass away "like an oil lamp being extinguished," with no residue of *kamma* remaining to cause further rebirth. He lives a useful life, dedicating himself to the service of mankind, yet he is not attached (in the sense of selfish grasping) to blame and praise, happiness or unhappiness. In this way he truly represents the ideals of a holy life.

## Two kinds of Sangha

The term Dhamma-Vinaya, used by the Buddha in reference to the religion he established, represents the two aspects of the Buddha's teachings, and these two aspects of the Buddha's teachings are the basic underlying principles for the two kinds of Sangha.

Vinaya or monastic discipline is said to be the mainstay of the religion (*vinayo sāsanassa āyu*). It is the principle on which the existence, the stability, and the development of the Conventional Sangha rest. A man, for instance, is admitted into membership of the monastic Order or Conventional Sangha through an ordination process prescribed by the Vinaya. He lives by the Vinaya rules. The Vinaya regulates his conduct both in regard to himself and in his interaction with others. His Dhamma practice is almost considered an extension of his effort to train according to the Vinaya, not a separate exercise in itself, and it is always kept in line with the Vinaya rules.

Thus the life of a Conventional Sangha member is essentially dependent upon the Vinaya. Obviously, this is also true of the Sangha as a community. Without the Vinaya, the whole structure of Conventional Sangha would collapse. It is in this sense that, according to Theravada Buddhism, the Vinaya is said to provide the mainstay for the religion.

The Dhamma, on the other hand, is the life and soul of the Noble Saṅgha, its essence, its inner quality. Just as Koṇḍañña entered into membership of the Noble Saṅgha through the realization of Dhamma, even so the existence of the Noble Saṅgha must necessarily rest on the Dhamma. Unlike Vinaya, the Dhamma has little to do with institutional or ceremonial procedures, although such things may provide a basic framework or support for its realization. The Dhamma also has a much broader application than the Vinaya and is equally important for both monks and the lay community. It places no restrictions with regard to individual status. Like monks, laypeople may practise the Dhamma and achieve, on their own virtue, admission into the Noble Saṅgha. This is purely a matter of personal training and self-development.

It is interesting to observe that, in response to a question whether there were noble disciples among the laity, the Buddha asserted that the number of his noble lay disciples was greater than that of monks. This very well demonstrates the universality of the Dhamma and how much opportunity is open to all seekers of the Truth to practise it. Of course, the monastic setting, with the disciplinary codes of conduct, provides an excellent ground for the cultivation of the Dhamma, especially for those who would otherwise find it difficult to practise or for practitioners whose temperaments favor a more structured environment. In fact, on a deeper level there exists a close link between these two aspects of the Buddha's teachings. The practice of the Vinaya facilitates progress in the Dhamma training, while progress in the Dhamma helps to put one at ease with the Vinaya. They are, so to say, two sides of the one coin.

## RELATIONSHIP BETWEEN THE NOBLE AND CONVENTIONAL SAṄGHAS

Like the Dhamma and the Vinaya, the Noble and the Conventional Saṅghas do not exclude one another. They are, in fact, more related to one another than may appear at first glance.

Within the framework of the Conventional Saṅgha, the Vinaya defines the roles and responsibilities of each member and also decides how members relate to one another. Respect is shown to another monk in accordance with seniority—those who were ordained later pay respect to those who received earlier ordination, even if it were a matter of hours or minutes. A monk of less than five years seniority, no matter how knowledgeable he may be, will have to live and train under his preceptor's or teacher's supervision. But within the Noble Saṅgha, recognition is given according to individuals' achievements in spiritual practice. An Arahant, though of younger age and seniority, receives greater respect and recognition than those worldlings (*puthujjana*), who are more advanced in age and seniority; a Non-Returner is considered more advanced than a Once-Returner in terms of spiritual achievement, and so forth.

However, since the Conventional Saṅgha is an institution, which must be governed by a defined set of rules and regulations, the Vinaya naturally takes precedence within it. The Vinaya provides a certain amount of consistency necessary for the smooth functioning and growth of the institution. It also helps to preserve peace and harmony among the members of the community. Thus a member of the Noble Saṅgha living within the context of the Conventional Saṅgha takes upon himself the responsibility of following the injunctions of the Vinaya, no matter how exalted his spiritual position may be. This may seem a little strange, but it is both practical and appropriate.

The Conventional Saṅgha, on the other hand, can look upon the Noble Saṅgha as the embodiment of virtues and religious ideals, whose presence provides a strong inspiration and encouragement for them to strive for the attainment of higher goals. The structured environments so well-grounded on the Vinaya should prove an advantage to Dhamma practice. Even members of the Noble Saṅgha who have not attained Arahantship may benefit from such environments. Moreover, while the Conventional Saṅgha is capable of creating excellent conditions to achieve membership in the Noble Saṅgha, it is the latter that will prove excellent members of the former and may, eventually, best preserve the institution of the former. In this way, the Noble and the Conventional Saṅghas complement one other.

Dhamma and Vinaya are reciprocally complementary and supportive. Just as a good person, well-educated and in high position, would endeavor to abide by the laws of the country, even so, advancement in the Dhamma by no means nurtures a contempt for the Vinaya. A noble disciple, though advanced in the Dhamma, recognizes the importance of the Vinaya in religious life. Because he has been able to remove most or all of the defilements, it becomes more natural for him to show respect for rules and regulations that are formulated for the common good of the community. Thus, whereas ordinary worldlings, who are still full of selfishness, greed, and pride, would at times find rules and laws cumbersome, especially when they are at variance with their interests, a noble disciple would feel at home with them.

In addition to preserving communal peace and harmony, the Vinaya is also of great value in the practice to realize the Dhamma. Progress in spiritual practice is not possible without self-discipline, and this can be inculcated through commitment to the Vinaya. On the other hand, as one becomes more advanced in the Dhamma, one will find it more natural to follow the Vinaya. In this way the Dhamma helps to maintain the Vinaya. Once a noble disciple reaches the highest stage of spiritual development, that is, Arahantship, and has no more training to do, he may no longer need the Vinaya for his own further progress, yet he will discern its value for the good of the community and will be willing to follow it with clear understanding and respect. There is abundant evidence to substantiate this in Buddhist canonical literature.

When Buddhism was first established, there were only Arahant disciples. The first group of sixty monks who spent the first rains residence (*vassa*) with the Buddha were all Arahants, and so were the more than one thousand disciples whom he taught on his way to the city of Rājagaha. It is said that on the full moon of the month of Māgha, barely seven months after he delivered the first discourse, a total of 1,250 monk disciples, who were directly ordained by him, assembled at the Bamboo Grove to see the Blessed One. They were also all Arahants.

To such highly accomplished disciples, the Buddha enjoined but one task: "Go forth, monks, for the welfare of the many, for the happiness of the many, out of compassion for the world, for the good, the benefit, and bliss of gods and men." The Buddha further said: "Released have you been from bondage, both human and divine. Teach, therefore, to the world the good Dhamma, which is beautiful in the beginning, beautiful in the middle, beautiful at the end." This was the mandate given by the Buddha for his disciples to carry the message of Dhamma to the masses, and it remains the driving principle underlying the Buddhist social philosophy even today.

Teachings given by the Buddha's noble disciples were most readily accepted. These disciples of the Buddha represented an ideal of spiritual training, demonstrating how a life of Dhamma should be lived and how the ultimate enlightenment can be achieved. Thanks partly to the efforts and dedication of these disciples, who were mostly monastic members, the religion of the Buddha became well established within a relatively short time.

For those monks who are not as yet fully enlightened there are two main duties to be carried out. The first is the duty of scriptural learning (*ganthadhura*), which familiarizes students with the doctrine and the discipline laid down by the Buddha, and gives them a proper direction and methodology for spiritual practice. The other duty is the training in meditation (*vipassanādhura*), which is the practical aspect of the higher religious life. Of course, even in the time of the Buddha, certain highly developed monks would engage themselves in scriptural learning, if only to help preserve the Buddha's words, just as they would engage in meditative exercises to experience the bliss of *Nibbāna*.

The institution of Saṅgha came into existence in response to the growing number of monks who came to join the Order. Definite structure took shape over the years. The primary function of the Saṅgha institution in its early days was to provide an ideal setting for the practice of Dhamma, where more energetic members could derive the benefits of moral support and instruction from good associates. Without such benefits the Saṅgha would be much less meaningful to the religious life it was originally intended to serve.

With the passage of time the role of the Saṅgha has expanded more and more into social concerns. Not only do monks teach Dhamma, they also perform ceremonies for the laity, especially at important events connected with life (such as births, weddings, and deaths). Their counsel is sought in family or communal disputes, their presence is considered auspicious at the opening ceremony of a new business, they are requested to bless a new house, a new office, or even a new car. In early Thailand, not only were monasteries seats of religious learning, even secular subjects were taught there until just before the introduction of the modern education system. Monks represented not only spiritual leadership n religious affairs, but also intellectual leadership in society, for they were usually the best educated sector of society. Because of the trust and confidence the community places in them, they are also looked up to for leadership in certain communal activities, especially in rural areas, where monks and laity enjoy closer bond and cooperation.

Monks' roles in society often reflect people's needs and their expectation of the Saṅgha institution. But foremost of all duties they are expected to fulfill are the two duties of scriptural learning and training in meditation.

## SAṄGHA AND SOCIAL WORK

The primary obligation of most novices and younger monks is to equip themselves for future religious assignments. This is only natural. If we do not expect young people studying in schools, colleges, and universities to shoulder heavy social responsibilities, it would be unfair to expect monk students to accomplish much when they are not yet well-equipped. Moreover, even while engaged in educational pursuits, the tasks and responsibilities these novices and young monks have to undertake are much more onerous than those of their lay counterparts. Not only do they study religious subjects, in which they specialize, they also have to study suitable secular subjects to supplement their religious knowledge in view of the duties they are expected to perform later on. In addition to this daunting challenge, they also have to work hard for "the welfare of the many, for the happiness of the many, out of compassion for the world." Because of their religious status, people always have high expectations and look up to them to fulfill those expectations. This is by no means an easy role and it often puts a considerable pressure on young monks.

Monks who are not burdened with educational careers do take an active part in religious and social concerns, especially if they are senior members of the Saṅgha. In fact, their responsibilities increase with age and seniority. At an age when most laymen would retire to enjoy their leisure, these elderly monks have to meet the increased expectations and demands that people have on them. Often they work hard until their last breath or until they become completely invalid, so great is their spirit of self-sacrifice and dedication. One of the reasons why this is not widely known to the public is because these selfless monks would rather keep to the tradition of silent service, quietly working for the benefit of others, than working to gain personal benefits and fame. Nevertheless, the fact remains that the social contributions made by the Saṅgha are, indeed, of inestimable value.

Today the monks' social roles are more visible in the rural areas or villages, where the bond between the Saṅgha and laity is still relatively unaffected by the urban culture and patterns of behavior. Poor villagers often turn to monks to mediate land disputes, family problems, and differences among neighbors. Unruly and stubborn children are taken to a monastery for training in discipline and other social values; sometimes boys are even ordained for that purpose. The village monastery also functions as the centre of social activities, where most communal affairs take place. When and where necessary, monks take initiative in various social projects, mainly by giving guidance and leadership, such as construction of schools and hospitals, roads and small reservoirs, and at times even the digging of a village well. They also take leadership in raising funds for such projects. In times of natural calamity there have been instances in which monks provided the most effective leadership in pooling resources together to help ameliorate the suffering of victims and their families.

Even forest monks, who are known for their natural inclination for meditation and solitude and who spend most of their lives in forests, contribute valuable services to society. They are looked upon with great respect and their counsel is sought after. They are either directly or, more often, indirectly instrumental in setting up charitable programs or foundations for the welfare of society. They help preserve the forests and water resources of the country. In most cases their influence and intervention in such matters prove more effective than those of government agencies. Again little or no efforts have been made to publicize their achievements and social contributions and a wider section of the public remains unaware of the fact.

In modern Thai society, although the new educational system has come to replace the traditional one, school facilities are often found located on monastic property donated by the Saṅgha. In addition to their assistance in raising funds for construction, monks also contribute their teaching skills in a number of those establishments. Naturally, monastery grounds where school facilities are located are often turned into playgrounds for the children. Noise and mischief spill into monastic environments. Good-naturedly, the monks put up with them and watch the children grow to become good and useful members of society.

### QUALIFICATIONS FOR ORDINATION

In the Theravada tradition, ordination as a nun (*bhikkhunī*) is no more available, but many women do receive religious vows and lead a monastic life akin to monks. They are often referred to as nuns. In Thailand most of these nuns dress in white (a few in dark brown) and are no less active than monks in religious and social activities. In Myanmar the usual color is very close to pink, while in Sri Lanka it is either yellow or saffron.

For male candidates there are two levels of ordination, the lower and the higher. A boy under twenty may request lower ordination and those who are twenty or more may request the higher one. Of course, those who are qualified for higher ordination, if they so desire, may request the lower one and remain in that position for as long as they wish, though that is not commonly practised.

A candidate for ordination must be physically fit, not handicapped or mentally defective. He must be in good health, physically as well as mentally. He must be free from contagious diseases such as leprosy, eczema, chloasma, and other dangerous chronic diseases such as epilepsy. Although venereal diseases and AIDS have not been mentioned in the Books of Discipline for obvious reasons, it is not unreasonable to assume that they do constitute a strong ground for rejection. Moreover, the candidate must have his parents' permission to be ordained, must have the king's permission, i.e., not bounded by government services, having duly taken leave, must be free of debt, and must be in possession of a bowl (for containing food) and a complete set of three robes.

The candidate desirous of ordination should be presented to the abbot of the monastery where he would like his ordination to take place by his parents or some of his senior relatives. He will be duly interviewed by the monk and, if found eligible, will be admitted to the monastery for preparatory training. Before the date of ordination he is expected to have mastered basic monastic rules and regulations as laid down by the Buddha and some fundamental knowledge in the Dhamma. The preceptor will also teach him monastic protocol and how he should conduct himself as a monk.

Questions about costs are usually a concern among Westerners, who are not accustomed to free services so common in the East, especially when religious matters are concerned. As a rule, services rendered by Buddhist monks or monasteries are without charge. The monasteries even provide free residential facilities. The only expenditure that is really needed for the ordination ceremony is that for the robes and bowl. A monk's life is meant to be austere, so there should be nothing other than what is needed for simple subsistence. Should the candidate find it difficult even to supply himself with those few items, the monastery may give him necessary support so as to enable him to fulfill his noble aspiration. Traditionally, the Buddha allowed only eight articles for monks' personal use. These are three robes, a (food) bowl, a razor, a needle, a cloth belt, and a water filter. Things other than these eight must be subjected to collective ownership of the whole monastic community to be distributed properly to needy members.

To receive ordination the candidate must first have his head shaved clean. This symbolizes his departure from the household life to homelessness. According to the Vinaya, a higher ordination ceremony may take place only in a specific building or area called *Uposatha* (the main chapel) of the monastery, which must be duly marked in all directions by boundary stones or some other solid objects. At least five monks must be present, including one who will act as the preceptor. In regions where monks are easily available, such as big cities, at least ten monks are required. The common practice in Thailand is to invite twenty monks to take part in the ceremony.

First the candidate approaches the monks, already assembled in the main chapel, with a set of robes and other requisites, accompanied by parents, relatives, and friends. Heading the chapter of monks present is the preceptor, usually the most senior and best qualified in the monastery. Sometimes a preceptor may be invited from another monastery to officiate over the ordination ceremony, if the candidate or his relatives so desire. Having approached the assembly of monks, the candidate prostrates before the preceptor and makes a formal request for ordination by reciting three times the Pali request passage. At the end of the recitation, he hands the set of robes over to his preceptor, who then proceeds to examine them to ascertain if they are proper for use.

Satisfied with the robes, the preceptor gives the candidate appropriate instruction concerning the life of a monk. He also explains some basic methods in meditation that involve contemplation on the impermanent and unsatisfactory nature of the five bodily objects: hair on the head, hair on the body, nails, teeth, and skin. Then he allows the candidate to put on the robes, assisted by one or two of the monks present. After putting on the robes the candidate again prostrates before his preceptor, or another senior monk appointed by him, and makes a request for the ten precepts of a novice. Part of this process involves going for refuge to the Triple Gem, at the conclusion of which the candidate is pronounced a novice (*sāmaṇera*). Then the new novice receives the ten precepts. The end of this precept administration marks the completion of the lower ordination ceremony.

The higher ordination ceremony continues from this point. The candidate makes a request for higher ordination to the Saṅgha by reciting the request passage three times. Thereupon, one or two monks (usually two) will be sanctioned by the Saṅgha present to question the candidate, who is now a novice, to ascertain his eligibility and readiness for monkhood. Special care is taken to ensure that the candidate is completely free from any conditions that would disqualify his entry into the monastic membership. This session is supposed to be carried out in private to allow total freedom for the interview, which therefore must be done outside the assembly. After questioning and being satisfied that the candidate is suitable for admission into the Saṅgha, the interviewers return to report their findings to the preceptor and other Saṅgha members.

After a proper consultation among the Saṅgha, the candidate is called into the assembly for cross-examination in their presence. The Saṅgha having been convinced of his eligibility, a motion is then proposed to the Saṅgha on the candidate's behalf requesting his admission into the institution. This motion is repeated three times to allow sufficient time for all the Saṅgha members to deliberate and raise objection should any of them feel strongly against the motion. Each Saṅgha member has equal right to vote for or against the candidate's proposed admission and a single objection would suffice to nullify the whole endeavor. In the absence of an objection, the motion will be carried, and the novice accepted as a member of the Saṅgha. From this point onward, the novice is elevated to the status of a fully-fledged monk, with all the duties and responsibilities of a Saṅgha member.

Before declaring the ceremony closed, the preceptor performs his last duty. He congratulates the new monk and gives him suitable instruction, especially that which concerns the most essential practice and rules of a monastic life. The ceremony usually concludes with the new monk performing an act of transferring merits to ancestors, parents, friends, well-wishers, and all other sentient beings. After that, relatives and other devotees make offerings to the new monk.

The whole procedure is conducted in the Pali language, except the instruction which the preceptor gives to the candidate at the beginning and the end of the ceremony.

## DAILY LIFE OF A MONK

The monastic life-style is very different from that of the laity. It is designed to be conducive to spiritual practice and suitable for a life of dedication and service. As such it has to be kept simple. It should also be free from family concerns and obligations. Whereas wealth is considered a symbol of success and social status, it is an impediment on the spiritual path, especially as far as monks are concerned. Monks' daily routines are also markedly different from those of lay people.

A monk's day begins in some monasteries as early as 3 a.m. By four most monks have already arisen. The predawn hours are devoted to meditation, chanting, and scriptural studies. At day-break, the monks walk the streets on almsround to receive food offerings from devotees. Monks in villages usually walk long distances, as houses there are few and far between. According to the Vinaya, monks may eat only between daybreak and midday, not before or after that. Some monks eat only one meal a day, others take breakfast and lunch, but all finish their last meal before midday.

Those monks who are engaged in educational activities spend the morning and afternoon sessions in educational pursuits, either teaching or studying as the case may be. Understandably, more educational facilities are found in urban areas or big cities. Some monasteries confine their curricula to religious subjects, such as those prescribed by ecclesiastical boards of education, others providing facilities for suitable secular subjects as well. Some monastic establishments specialize in Abhidhamma, which represents the metaphysical aspects of the Buddha's teachings.

Monks living in meditation centres spend a good part of their time each day on meditative practices. Late afternoon session is normally reserved for collective manual labor, where all monastic inmates, monks or lay practitioners, join hands to fulfil their monastic chores, such as sweeping the compounds, cleaning the main chapel, drawing water from the well, etc. Those who live in community monasteries are also prone to engage in social welfare activities; they teach in schools, give counsel, or visit the sick. They are also often invited to perform ceremonies in houses or at business establishments. More gifted monks may write books, or give lectures at universities.

Normally, there are two services of worship each day, morning and evening. Morning services may be conducted either in the early dawn or after breakfast, evening services take place around the early hours of the evening. As a rule, in forest monasteries, where special emphasis is on meditation, morning services are conducted in the early hours of dawn, e.g. around 3:30 or 4:00, and evening services begin around 7:00 or 7:30. These services consist mainly of chanting and a period of sitting meditation. Occasionally, senior monks give instruction and long discourses on the Dhamma or meditation. Shorter discourses are more regular. Those monks who are as yet students devote the night hours to scriptural learning and homework. By the time they retire, it is already late in the night.

Monasteries in Thailand are in a perpetual process of building, expansion, and renovation and it is not uncommon to see construction activities going on at any time of the year, even in monasteries which have been founded for decades. In many instances, construction labor comes from monks and novices living in the monasteries themselves, particularly those in villages. The monks are thus kept busy all year round.

Though the monks' life is simple, it is never idle. With all the duties and responsibilities they are expected to fulfil, both as individual members of the Saṅgha and as spiritual leaders of the community, monks exemplify the spirit of the Buddha's mandate by dedicating themselves to the welfare and happiness of the world.

## SHAVING THE HEAD

The shaving of the hair symbolizes renunciation and marks one's departure from the worldly life. This is clearly one of the most striking physical distinctions between a monk and a householder, indicating the monk's changed status. Since monastic life is meant to be simple and burden-free, shaving the head helps to realize that objective. Hair is an object of vanity and pride, qualities that are not supportive of spiritual practice. Thus monks are advised to shave and keep the hair short. In Thailand monks and novices all over the country keep to the tradition of shaving their heads on the same day of every lunar month, on the full moon eve. This tradition is not observed in other Theravada countries, although the practice of shaving and keeping the hair short is commonly followed by all monks—Theravada, Mahayana, and Vajrayana—the world over.

Since shaving strongly represents the values of a religious life, monks and novices are encouraged to meditate, during the tonsure, on the transitory and unsatisfactory nature of the hair. They are also reminded to reflect on the duties and responsibilities that a religious life, so vividly symbolized by the cut hair, has enjoined on them. There are reports of some spiritually advanced disciples during the Buddha's time who attained Arahantship while shaving. Thus, the simple act can be used as a means to attain higher and nobler objectives.

Like the hair, monks' robes are also meant to reflect the

simplicity and austerity of religious life. In the earlier part of the Buddha's mission, when the number of monks was relatively small, the only way that a monk could get a robe was by collecting castaway pieces of cloth, wherever they could be found. These were thoroughly cleaned, boiled, dyed, and stitched together to make a larger piece, sufficient for the purpose. It was the intention of the Buddha not to create burdens for the lay community by asking for their support in this regard. Even the dye was obtained by boiling down suitable wood or bark. The Buddha wanted monks to be as self-sufficient as possible and learn to be content with little (*appicchatā*). A monk is expected to keep only three main robes at a time as part of his eight requisites; these robes consisting of an under robe, an upper robe, and an outer robe. They are simply cloths of rectangular shape, made up from many smaller pieces, and the pattern of stitching "following the pattern of the Magadha paddy fields" has been maintained down to the present, even when textiles are available in abundance. This explains why monks' robes have the patchy appearance they do today.

The color of the monks' robes is brownish yellow, although the shades may differ. Forest monks are often distinguished by the darker shade of their robes, but some monks living in villages or cities may also use similar color (although their usual tone is a lighter one).

## MONASTIC RULE

There are ten principal precepts and seventy-five minor rules for novices (those of lower ordination), and these rules define how they should conduct themselves in matters concerning the use of their robes and proper social etiquette, how food should be accepted and consumed, the manner in which a discourse should be delivered, and miscellaneous behavioral expressions.

For a fully-fledged monk there are much more numerous rules

and regulations. Most important are the 227 rules that are contained in a book called *Pāṭimokkha*. Of these 227 rules and regulations, four are the most serious, transgression of them resulting in permanent expulsion from the Saṅgha. Others are considered 'redeemables.' Monks who have committed a redeemable disciplinary breach are required to confess to the Saṅgha, a group of monks, or an individual monk. Thirteen of these redeemable offences necessitate a period of probation, during which the offender undergoes a meditative retreat and engages in a process of self-examination, before he will be considered for readmission by a panel of no less than twenty Saṅgha members.

Theravada Buddhism endeavors to preserve all the Vinaya rules and regulations exactly as they were laid down by the Buddha more than twenty-five centuries ago, neither adding any new ones nor rejecting the existing ones. This decision was taken at the First Buddhist Council, held three months after the Buddha passed away, and it is still honored today. Of course, individual monasteries may enforce rules and regulations of their own, but such measures must not conflict with the Vinaya. Moreover, they may be subjected to alteration or modification from time to time, but the Vinaya will always remain untouched and unchanged. This is the true spirit of the Theravada tradition.

# 6

# KAMMA

## What is Kamma?

ETYMOLOGICALLY, THE PALI WORD *KAMMA* (Sanskrit: *karma*) is derived from the root "kar" meaning "to do," "to commit," or "to perform." *Kamma* literally means action, something we do or perform. But according to the Buddhist philosophy, not all actions are designated *kamma*; only those actions that are volitionally motivated are called *kamma*. The Pali word for volition is *cetanā*. It is the most crucial conditioning factor behind human actions and determines the nature of such actions. The Buddha has clearly explained: "Monks, volition do I call *kamma*. Having willed, man commits *kamma* through body, speech, and mind." In his *Abhidhammasamuccaya*, Asaṅga, an eminent Mahayana commentator, defines volition as "mental construction or mental activity, the function of which is to direct the mind in the sphere of virtuous, evil, and neutral activities."

The doctrine of *kamma* is based on the principle of causality or the law of cause and effect. It is the natural law of morality, which asserts that an intentional action will lead to a result proportionate in nature and intensity to that intention. Karmically productive actions are those which are based on skillful or unskillful volition. The Pali word for skillful is *kusala*, which is variously translated as wholesome, good, meritorious, virtuous, and intelligent. The Pali word for unskillful is *akusala*, translated as unwholesome, evil, bad, deleterious, unvirtuous, and unintelligent. A skillful action produces a result which is desirable, good, and happy, while an unskillful deed brings about just the opposite. As the Buddha has eloquently declared : "Just as the seed is sown, so will the fruit be obtained. The doer of good receives good; the doer of evil receives evil."

Often the word *kamma* is used not only in reference to an intentional action, but also, wrongly, to indicate the result thereof. This kind of confusion is common even among the educated, not to mention the untrained, who tend to be rather indiscreet in their choice of terms. *Kamma* means an action, never its result. The Pali words for the result are *phala*, *vipāka*, or *kammavipāka*. It is important to be aware of this distinction to avoid misunderstandings about *kamma*.

Skillful or unskillful intention constitutes the motivation underlying the performance of an action. When there is an intention to perform *kamma*, there arises volitional energy that provides a moving force for the action, whether wholesome or unwholesome, depending on the kind of volition at the moment. This action may be expressed through any of the three channels of body, speech, and mind. In fact, it is intention that conditions man's action and constitutes the basis for all mental formations.

## THE LAW OF KAMMA AND MORAL JUSTICE

The law of *kamma* has nothing to do with the idea of moral justice. Although some scholars try to claim their common origin or confuse them through analogy, there is no justification for such efforts. To begin with, the theory of moral justice is grounded on the assumption of a supreme being or a so-called creator God, the lawgiver who sits in judgement over all actions. It is he who is believed to mete out justice, giving punishment to sinners and rewards to believers as the case may be. But the meaning of the expression 'moral justice' in theistic religions is ambiguous, and history has shown that much injustice has been made in the name of moral justice. The criteria for defining moral justice are, to say the least, rather arbitrary and subjective. Often they serve only as a pretext for righteous bigotry and political opportunism, with decidedly self-defeating effects.

The law of kamma, on the other hand, is a natural law. It is a law of cause and effect, of action and reaction. The law of kamma operates on its own, requiring no assumption of a God, and has nothing to do with the idea of reward or punishment. In fact the concept of justice is irrelevant, a mere expedient in the cause of convenience of expression, a convention. Of course, the law of kamma operates with full and perfect justice, but that is quite a different matter from the concept of justice as understood in theistic religions. When the Buddha says, "The doer of good receives good, the doer of evil receives evil," he is not passing a judgement of reward or punishment, but simply stating the fact of how the law of kamma operates. If you fall down from a tree and break your leg, it is not a matter of justice or punishment, but simply the operation of the law of gravity, a natural law which we all are subject to. Likewise, if you eat good food and remain healthy, your health is only natural, not a reward given to you by some supreme being. Whether a supreme being exists or not, you will remain healthy and strong if you treat yourself properly in accordance with the law of nature. Of course, we may refer to the broken leg as a punishment and good health as a reward, but that is just a way of talking. The law of kamma operates in much the same manner, the difference being that it functions within the framework of morality, based on the principle of cause and effect.

There are those who assert that it is God who made all these laws, and if the law of *kamma* were true, it must also have been created by God. We can see that the introduction of God into the subject only serves to confuse and obscure the issue. Historically, the Buddhist doctrine of *kamma* was first condemned by Christians as the teaching of Satan, or a heretic view at best. However, with better understanding and the subsequent realization of the sound logic and validity of this particular doctrine, some Christian scholars have compromised by reducing it to one of the 'Laws' established by the 'Father in Heaven.' This maneuver calls to mind the practice of Hindus of old who first condemned the Buddha and later reduced him to one of Vishnu's incarnations. But since the existence of God is as yet a matter of conjecture, such a claim does not hold much weight and may serve only to divert us from pursuing the subject in the right direction.

## RESULTS OF KAMMA

*Kamma* can be committed through the three doors or channels of action: actions done through the body, such as giving things in charity, killing, stealing, or taking narcotic drugs, are called bodily actions (*kāyakamma*); those performed through speech, such as telling the truth, lying, or using abusive language, are called verbal actions (*vacīkamma*); those performed through the mind, such as indulging in hateful thoughts or practising concentration and insight meditation, are called mental actions (*manokamma*).

Most people do not see thoughts as a kind of action and fail to realize how they can be anything more than mere subjective phenomena. But it is interesting to note that Buddhism not only lists the function of the mind as constituting a kind of action, but gives it prime significance. According to Buddhism, it is through mental action that man can be elevated to the highest stage of spiritual development, and it is again through mental action that he will be tempted to commit the most heinous crime. Thus cultivation of mind occupies the most important place in the Buddhist scheme of spiritual training.

A volitional action, good or bad, skillful or unskillful, is bound to produce some appropriate result one way or another. Sometimes the consequences of an action are immediate and explicit; sometimes they are not. This really depends on many factors. Some actions may bear fruit in the present life, others may bring results in some future lifetime. However, the most immediate and obvious result of an intentional action can be observed at the time the deed is committed. A good deed, for instance, results in the doer being a good individual, and a bad action renders him a bad one. This is the law of *kamma* in operation right at the time an action is performed, which can be empirically experienced.

Says the Buddha: "All sentient beings are the owners of their *kamma*, inheritors of their *kamma*, born of their *kamma*, related to their *kamma*, supported by their *kamma*. *Kamma* is that which divides beings into coarse and refines states."

## DETERMINING THE QUALITY OF ACTIONS

We have seen that intention, according to the Buddha's teachings, constitutes *kamma*. In English, we tend to use the term 'intention' rather loosely to indicate our willingness or purpose in an action. For instance, we may say, "I intend to write home" or "He said it intentionally." Sometimes, intention is implicit in the inference even if the word is not used. "He looks at the picture" clearly indicates an intention involved in the act of looking. However, intention in such instances contains no specific moral implication and the actions so performed do not fall into either the wholesome or unwholesome category, but are of an indeterminate nature.

This is the point of distinction. The Abhidhamma classifies

intention or volition as a mental concomitant (*cetasika*) that is present in all types of consciousness. There is no consciousness that arises without it. Volition has the function of assisting the mind to select objects of awareness. By nature it is morally indeterminate, but becomes qualified as wholesome or unwholesome in accordance with the wholesome or unwholesome mental concomitants which arise with it. It is on the basis of these factors that an action is determined as morally good or bad. Of course, for the sake of convenience we may refer to a particular element of intention as skillful or unskillful volition, but the Abhidhamma analyses this down to the very fundamental qualities of each and every individual type of consciousness.

A simple indeterminate action may turn into a morally skillful or unskillful one depending on associated factors. With the accompaniment of wholesome mental qualities, an otherwise morally neutral action will be transformed into a wholesome one. If the accompanying mental qualities are unwholesome, the opposite will result. If we understand this rather intricate relationship between the action and the mental states at the time the action is carried out, there will be no difficulty in determining the moral implication of our own actions in everyday life.

We may further clarify this through an illustration. Take, for instance, the simple act of eating or drinking. Ordinarily, this in itself cannot be classified as morally good or bad and is, therefore, not karmically productive. However, such ordinary actions are bound to become either morally wholesome or unwholesome if and when founded on, or accompanied by, wholesome or unwholesome mental qualities (with volition playing an important supportive role).

Eating with mindfulness and clarity of mind as a form of meditative practice is wholesome because it is accompanied by awareness and wisdom, which are positively wholesome mental qualities. Such an act is therefore a morally good action. Drinking intoxicants that cloud the mind and produce heedlessness is morally unwholesome, as is borne out by the crime and violence that are associated with such consumption. Its effect is much different from drinking a glass of pure water.

All actions lead to certain results; every action produces a reaction. If you walk, you get to a certain place; if you eat, you get full; if you lie down and close your eyes, you will fall asleep. But the Buddhist doctrine of *kamma* does not concern these morally indeterminate actions because they have no ethical implication and have little to do with moral training. However, these very same ordinary actions are potentially good or bad from the moral standpoint if and when they are accompanied by respective moral or immoral volition. With understanding they may be employed for the purpose of moral development or even for spiritual practice. The teachings of *kamma* concern those volitional actions, including walking, eating, and sleeping, which bear moral significance and provide the ground for moral consideration and cultivation.

## DEFINING GOOD AND EVIL

Sometimes the terms 'good' and 'evil' are used to translate the Pali *kusala* and *akusala*, but students should also be aware of the fine points of distinction that exist between them and keep in mind those differences when referring to specific instances concerning Buddhist ethical values. For example, detachment, being content with little, and renunciation are considered *kusala*, but they are not necessarily good for most people; melancholy, attachment, and worry are *akusala*, but they are not generally taken to be evil. Even greed, positively an *akusala* state, may often be considered good by some, say, in business and politics. The concepts of good and evil have something to do with social values, whereas *kusala* and *akusala* are more connected to the inner qualities of the mind. That is why non-judgemental terms like 'wholesome' or 'unwholesome' are more preferable. If 'good' and 'evil' are used, they should be used with due caution and awareness.

*Kusala* and *akusala* are mental qualities, which initially affect the conditions of the mind. From this source of actions, *kamma* is performed through the body, the speech, or the mind itself. Thus wholesome or unwholesome actions are generally determined by the condition or the contents of the mind. Buddhist commentators define *kusala* as being characterized by 1) a healthy mind which is free from illness and affliction (*arogya*); 2) a clear mind which is untarnished and unstained (*anavajja*); 3) a judicious mind imbued with wisdom and knowledge (*kosalasambhūta*); and a content and happy mind which has well-being as its reward (*sukhavipāka*). The definition of *akusala* is directly opposite to that of *kusala* for it is associated with the mind that is weak and unhealthy, harmful, ignorant (lacking in knowledge and understanding), and resulting in pain and suffering.

Thus *kusala* represents the mental conditions that promote mental quality, and *akusala* is that which causes mental degeneration and brings down the quality and efficiency of the mind.

## EXAMPLES OF WHOLESOME AND UNWHOLESOME KAMMA

If we understand the explanation given above, there will be no problem distinguishing wholesome from unwholesome actions. In general we may say that such positive actions as charity, meditation, and supporting one's parents are wholesome, and negative actions such as quarrelling, stealing, and making fun of others are unwholesome. This is almost a matter of common sense. Nevertheless, for the sake of further clarity in the subject we may refer to the Buddha's teachings on the ten unwholesome actions and the corresponding wholesome ones:

There are three unwholesome actions that are performed through body, namely, killing, taking what is not given, and indulgence in sexual misconduct. There are four kinds of verbal actions which are unwholesome: false speech, malicious or slanderous speech, harsh speech, and frivolous speech. There are three kinds of unwholesome mental actions: covetousness, ill will, and false view. In nature and content, these last three are closely identified with the three roots of unskillful action, namely, greed, anger, and ignorance. Other examples of unwholesome *kamma* may include the following mental concomitants as well as their resultant actions through body, speech and mind: greed or desire for sensual pleasure, dejection, sloth and torpor, restlessness and anxiety, uncertainty of mind or lack of resolution, jealousy, avarice, and miserliness.

On the wholesome side, there are also ten skillful actions, three bodily, four verbal, and three mental, consisting of abstention from the ten unwholesome actions mentioned above. Wholesome actions depicted in this way are somewhat negative, at least in tone, through the use of the Pali word *veramaṇī*, which means 'abstention.' But a negative expression does not necessarily mean a negative state of mind or action. Abstention from false speech, for instance, is a negative expression, but it also implies a positive commitment, since such abstention itself naturally signifies truthfulness. Refraining from stealing not only specifies that one should avoid such an act, but also implies a positive quality of respect for others' property rights.

The Buddha pointed out how the ten wholesome actions can be followed in both the negative and positive aspects. This may be listed as follows:

1. Abstaining from destruction of life, one cultivates loving-kindness and compassion, working for the welfare of all beings.

2. Abstaining from taking what is not given, one cultivates respect for others' property rights and earns a livelihood through fair means.

3. Abstaining from sexual misconduct, one practises self-restraint and observes good morals.

4. Abstaining from false speech, one adheres to truth, is honest and trustworthy.

5. Abstaining from malicious speech, one endeavors to reconcile people and promote harmony among community members.

6. Abstaining from harsh language, one practises pleasant and courteous speech.

7. Abstaining from frivolous speech, one speaks only speech which is useful, reasonable, and appropriate to the listener, time, and purpose.

8. Abstaining from covetous thoughts, one practises generosity and altruism.

9. Abstaining from thoughts of ill will, one cultivates goodwill and kind thoughts toward all beings, wishing them freedom from fear and suffering.

10. Abstaining from wrong view, one develops right understanding and right conviction in the law of *kamma*, believing in the fruits of wholesome and unwholesome actions.

Some of the more obvious examples of *kusala* mental qualities include concentration, mindfulness, calm, non-arrogance or humility, desire for that which is good (*kusalachanda*), joy in the Dhamma, and insight in the realization of Truth.

## CRITERIA OF WHOLESOME AND UNWHOLESOME ACTIONS

Generally, this may be just a matter of common sense for most people. Any judicious person can tell whether an action is wholesome or unwholesome, good or evil. According to Buddhism, it is action which defines a person as good or evil. We are what *kamma* makes of us.

However, in an age when there is a universal clamor for individual rights and freedom of expression, ethical concepts such as right and wrong, good and evil, are consistently reduced to a matter of mere personal opinions and social preferences. Logical positivism, a 20th century philosophical school, for instance, asserts that metaphysical theories and ethical propositions are fundamentally meaningless because a valid statement must be characterized either by its analytical property and conclusive verifiability, or at least by its being capable of confirmation through empirical experiment and observation.

So it is relevant here to point out that Buddhist ethical thoughts and values are not mere personal opinions or social preferences, but represent solid reality connected with human life and are based on the principle of moral causality.

Firstly, there is the consideration from the perspective of the consequences of a given action. That action is wholesome which produces a wholesome result and brings about happiness and benefit to oneself and others. If an action results in unhappiness and harm, if it causes loss and negative results, then it is an unwholesome or bad action. Says the Buddha: "On account of whatever *kamma* one experiences distress, pain and distraction, that is unskillful *kamma*. On account of whatever *kamma* one experiences no distress (negative outcome), but a heart bright and full of joy, that is skillful *kamma*." Thus a good or evil action may be determined on the basis of results. The Buddha adds, "Realizing what *kamma* is beneficial, one should, therefore, strive to act accordingly without delay."

Secondly, we can also determine whether a *kamma* is wholesome or unwholesome on the basis of its mental properties. If an action is based on any of the three wholesome roots (*kusalamūla*), then it is a wholesome action, but if it is rooted in any of the three unwholesome qualities (*akusalamūla*), then it is an unwholesome action. These so-called 'roots' are, in fact, mental concomitants, qualities of mind that accompany the consciousness at the moment an action is committed. Each moment of consciousness is characterized as wholesome or unwholesome according to the accompanying mental concomitants. The three unwholesome roots are greed (*lobha*), anger (*dosa*), and delusion (*moha*). The

The three wholesome roots are non-greed (*alobha*), non-anger (*adosa*), and non-delusion (*amoha*). Just as a tree is fed by its roots, a person's actions are also determined by the nature of these fundamental mental qualities that are associated with them.

## BELIEF IN KAMMA

The law of *kamma* operates universally, with absolute impartiality, and all are bound to experience its effects. There is no discrimination whatsoever with regard to race, sex, social status, or religious beliefs. However, one needs to be reminded that what is involved in a single act of omission or commission may be more than just the direct kammic factors of, say, a physical action and wholesome or unwholesome qualities of mind. Thus, in many cases the resultant consequences of a more objective nature may not be immediately apparent. For instance, due to certain factors involved a murderer may be able to escape the hand of law for some time, which may give him a false sense of relief and security. However, the Buddha has given us the express assurance that, "All *kamma*, whether wholesome or unwholesome, will bear fruit. There is no *kamma*, no matter how insignificant, which is without fruit." He has also said: "As long as an evil deed is not yet ripened, the evil one may perceive his evil deed as sweet as honey. But when it ripens, he will come to grief."

So, although religious beliefs may be an important factor in motivating moral actions, the consequences thereof do not depend on beliefs or conviction. If a man falls from a tree, he will experience the effect of the fall just the same, whether he is Buddhist or Moslem. Likewise, eating good and healthy food gives us the necessary nourishment, no matter what religion we may follow. A good or evil action is bound to bring about a good or bad result, as the case may be, regardless of the religion of the perpetrator of that action. This is the universality of the Dhamma.

## KAMMA AND PREDESTINATION

For a theory to be scientifically sound, it needs to be formulated on a scientific method. This involves procedures for seeking knowledge based on a recognition of problems or hypotheses, collection of data through systematic experiment and observation, and formulation of a rational theory. By now the time-honored Buddhist law of *kamma*, with its attendant doctrine of rebirth, has already been accepted by many of the world's leading intellectuals as logical and scientific. Professor Carl Gustav Jung, the eminent psychologist, has conceded that it is something worthy of serious study. He observed: "As a student of comparative religion, I believe that Buddhism is the most perfect one the world has ever seen. The philosophy of the Buddha, the theory of evolution, and the law of *kamma* were far superior to any other creed."

The law of *kamma* is a direct result of the Buddha's enlightenment. Even from the perspective of common sense there is hardly any principle more logical than the law of *kamma*, which postulates that good actions beget good results and bad actions beget bad ones. Ethically, this seems to be the only sound and tenable proposition.

One can observe and experiment with the law of *kamma* with one's own sense faculties and reasoning powers. Let us suppose, for instance, that we start smoking an occasional cigarette. An unskillful *kamma* has been committed. Now we can observe the changes (results of *kamma*) that are taking place as we continue to repeat the unskillful action. Smoking one cigarette acts as a potential for our indulgence in the next. As a result, a taste for tobacco, an inclination, and the habit to smoke develop, leading finally to addiction. By looking closely at the whole process, we will be able to see how we experience results proportionate to the actions that we have wilfully committed.

*Kamma* may also be understood in term of impulses. Smoking builds up impulses, both psychological and physical, and compels us to smoke even more until it becomes habitualized. The same is true with other more subtle actions. When we are annoyed or irritated, we may choose either to use this opportunity to practice kindness and transform our annoyance into a more positive experience, or we may act out our negative emotion and express anger through some physical or verbal action. Any course of action we undertake is a potential for further similar reaction under similar circumstances. By repeatedly practising to transform anger to kindness, we can develop a kindly nature and cheerful character. On the other hand, if we repeatedly shout at someone every time we get angry, that *kamma* will result in transforming us into hot-tempered and quarrelsome people. This is how we can empirically observe and experiment with the law of *kamma*, and see for ourselves how this law of cause and effect, action and reaction, operates in our daily lives. Based on this principle, we can expand the fields of our observation and experiment to increase our knowledge and understanding of *kamma*. Of course, the most comprehensive and infallible method is naturally the one employed by the Buddha and his noble disciples, which involves the special psychic instruments of higher spiritual knowledge.

The law of *kamma* is different from the idea of fatalism or predetermination. In fact, Buddhism rather talks about causal relationships than things being predetermined. The *Aṅguttara Nikāya* mentions three views which Buddhism does not subscribe to. The first is past-action determinism, which asserts that all our experiences in the present life are solely determined by past actions. The second is theistic determinism, which means that all our experiences and all events are due to God's creation and will. And the third view rejected by the Buddha is called accidentalism, which holds that all experiences are merely manifestations of fortuitous elements, uncaused and unconditioned. This fallacious view rejects the principle of causality and the law of *kamma*.

The first two views allow no room for free will, and are fatalistic in nature. The third is obviously untenable for the simple reason that it goes directly against common sense and the well-established truth of causal relationship. Buddhism advocates the middle course with the law of *kamma*, which states that our experiences are conditioned by our actions rather than being predetermined or willed by God. It realistically allows for a plurality of causes or conditioning factors, including the factors of will and natural phenomena. In this way the Buddhist doctrine of *kamma* seems most sensible and has a strong appeal for modern critical minds.

### DEVELOPMENT OF KAMMIC IMPULSES

When an action is performed through body, speech, or mind, there is always some energy involved. This energy is capable of being fortified, developed, or transformed. If a given action is repeatedly committed, the energy to commit the same deed will be strengthened, and consequently a tendency and habit will be formed. It is this tendency to habituation that makes it possible to train and develop both positive and negative tendencies. For example, by consistently practising meditation, we will find that the practice becomes more and more natural to us and we gradually cultivate the tendency and habit to meditate with greater ease. A person who repeatedly practices generosity develops the energy of giving and is therefore better prepared to give even more. The first act of giving may be difficult, if only because one is not used to it, but the first gift makes the second and subsequent ones easier, for it acts as the potential for a more advanced development of personal character. In the same way, if one repeatedly indulges in lying, it will become a habit. The first act of lying contains within itself the potential for lying the second time, and the third, and the fourth, until one becomes a compulsive liar. Habits are not physical, but they manifest themselves through physical actions. Understanding the law of *kamma* helps us to see the possibility of free choice and how we are truly responsible for our actions. We will also perceive that it is always within our capacity to train ourselves, to undo negative habits and cultivate positive ones.

Each and every person is comprised of five aggregates, which are corporeality, feeling, perception, mental formations, and consciousness. These are all different forms of energy, compounded, co-dependent, and co-functioning in the ever-changing flow of life. They represent a complex entity of fundamental elements which are interdependent and interrelated. Some of these forms of energy are gross, others are more subtle and refined. The energy of *kamma* is a more forceful part of mental formations and is thus intricately interwoven with all other forms of energy. Previous *kamma* therefore plays an important role in influencing later actions, though not necessarily the only one. The continuity of the five aggregates, supported by various conditioning factors, signifies the possibility of a life process without the intervention of a soul element, and ensures the uninterrupted continuation and operation of *kamma*.

## KAMMA FROM PREVIOUS LIVES

The mind stream which flows from moment to moment through life, continually rising and falling, carries within itself the conditioned potential of a person's personality, temperament, likes, dislikes, and all other mental constructions and impressions. Although these potentialities exist in a state of constant flux and are subject to the laws of change and conditionality, each successive moment of consciousness, with all its mental corollaries, is conditioned by its preceding moment. This process continues throughout the present life and passes on to the next in an unbroken stream. What we are now is therefore, to a large extent, inherited from what we were in the past. This partly helps to explain why we characteristically possess certain inclinations and attitudes and why we sometimes have an inexplicably strong like or dislike for certain individuals we encounter for the first time.

Based on the doctrine of *kamma*, it is possible to understand the present in reference to the past and to foresee the future through inference from the present. But this is no more a foregone conclusion than the statement, "We are what we were." Predetermination is not a Buddhist idea, neither is fate, destiny, or accidentalism. *Kamma* is open to the influence of conditioning factors, both in the present as well as the future. Even conditioned impulses, which hold the makings of the future, are subject to the influence of free will, that is, whether or not we choose to act on them. For example, an alcoholic is offered a bottle of whiskey: he experiences an impulse to drink. Based on past observation, we can predict with a high degree of probability that he would lose no time in emptying its contents into his stomach. Although that seems to be the most natural course of action, yet at that critical moment he still has the choice whether to act on the impulse or resolve to fight back by denying himself the unwholesome drink. In other words, he is not totally predetermined to consume the whiskey. *Kamma* could be influenced by other physio-psychological conditions as well.

One Buddhist meditation technique involves constant awareness of one's own thoughts. This is the most effective way to check the constantly changing states of mind, to see clearly how impulses arise, and how they are conditioned. By giving ourselves more space to reflect and contemplate, we will be able to get in touch with our own inner nature and our weaknesses and strengths. Most importantly, this awareness enables us to make better choices, to deal directly with our own impulses, not only by acting them out in a beneficial manner, but transforming them, if they are negative, to positive ones. Mindfulness helps us to make wise decisions with regard to our impulses so that we are not tempted to perform unwholesome actions, but rather engage in wholesome ones.

Our interest and receptivity to the Dhamma can also be explained according to the law of *kamma*. In fact, the existence of child prodigies can also be rationalized on the basis of the law of *kamma*, together with the Buddhist teachings on rebirth. It is likely that if we had studied and practised the Dhamma in our previous lives, we would be more inclined to do so in the present. If we had mastered the subject in the past, it is natural that we should find it easy in the present. By extension, this principle is also cited to explain why some children are so extraordinarily receptive to certain subjects, and not to others. They study them as if they had thoroughly understood them in the past and are merely revising what had been previously mastered.

## OTHER CONDITIONING FACTORS

The law of nature has been explained by Buddhist commentators as consisting of five distinct aspects. Underlying all these aspects is the principle of causal dependence and its expression in various modes of relationship. All things exist and operate, or cease to exist, in accordance with these five aspects of the law of nature. They are the principles by which the world and all its phenomena are regulated and controlled. The Pali term is *niyāma*, which literally means 'certainty,' the fixed order of nature. According to this, specific conditions inevitably determine certain corresponding results or effects, and each determinant may simultaneously interact with the others and be likewise determined by them.

The first aspect of the natural law is its physical inorganic order (*utuniyāma*). This concerns physical phenomena that take place on account of natural conditions, such as seasonal cycles, heat and cold, rain or snow, flowers blooming in spring and drying up in time of drought, and wax melting with the heat and hardening with the cold.

The second is that of the physical organic order (*bījaniyāma*), which refers to the natural law pertaining to heredity, the transmission of hereditary character and the genetic processes. The natural law of physical organic order can be observed in such phenomena as how a particular kind of tree grows from a certain seed, how fruits taste according to their species, how children bear physical resemblances to their parents, and how animals, birds, and insects, look, live, reproduce, and behave in certain ways according to their species.

The third aspect of natural law concerns the nature and functions of mind (*cittaniyāma*), such as the mental perception of sense-objects, the experience of sensations, the various mental processes that take place from moment to moment, the rising and cessation of consciousness, the attributes of mind and mental concomitants, hypnotic experiences, and mental states in varying levels of development.

The fourth aspect of natural law is a moral one. This is the principle of *kamma*, or the law of action and result (*kammaniyāma*). It specifically refers to the process of volitional activities and explains how certain actions lead to corresponding consequences, why people are born with certain peculiarities of character, and human behavior in the context of mental construction and proliferation. The law of *kamma* is based on the axiomatic principle that all actions inevitably lead to results proportionate in nature and degree to the deed.

The fifth aspect of natural law is the order of the norm, the all-encompassing law of causality and conditionality (*dhammaniyāma*) that regulates and controls all phenomena and governs the interrelatedness and interdependence of all things. This order of the norm is manifest in how things change and decay, how life is characterized by birth, old age, disease and death, how all existential realities are marked by the three characteristics of impermanence, unsatisfactoriness, and non-substantiality, how the law of gravity operates, how the sun rises in the east and sets in the west, how the whole cosmic order exists and functions, and so on.

As can be seen, *kamma* constitutes but one aspect of natural law. The simplistic supposition that all life experiences are due to *kamma* is therefore incorrect. Understanding these different underlying elements in the physical and psychical spheres helps us to gain a clearer understanding of how a single event may have resulted from more than one cause and how different determinants may synchronously be involved in conditioning certain phenomena or experiences. Usually, when more than one principle is at work, the more predominant one will prevail. For example, extreme temperature (*utuniyāma*) may influence the conditions of the mind (*cittaniyāma*) and cause one to feel ill at ease. Or strong will power (*cittaniyāma*) may temporarily override the effects of negative environments (*utuniyāma*) and the results of *kamma* (*kammaniyāma*).

## KAMMA AND NOT-SELF

The law of *kamma* does not necessarily presuppose the existence of a permanent self. On the contrary, it indicates the negation of self, as we shall presently discuss.

The idea of a permanent self is conceived on a psychologically deep-rooted fear of death and annihilation. To maintain a sense of security and ensure self-preservation, the false concept of an immortal soul, believed to be unchanging and eternal, is created. But according to the law of causal dependence, this concept is untenable and unwarranted because all things, animate or inanimate, are relative and must depend on certain conditions for their arising and existence. Since all things are conditioned, it follows that they are also liable to change and disintegrate according to the conditions on which they depend.

Instead of the soul theory, the Buddha taught the doctrine of no-soul or nonself (Pali: *anattā*). According to this doctrine, such a thing as soul or self is illogical and impossible. It is a false concept which bears no relation to reality, and is a prolific breeding ground for defilements such as selfishness, conceit, attachment, hatred, and desire. The Buddha's philosophical position is unique in the history of human thought for he unequivocally rejects the concept of soul which had previously been unquestioningly accepted. The Buddhist doctrine of nonself stands firm on the ground of sound logic and good reason, and is completely compatible with the law of *kamma*.

To begin with, self and *kamma* are two reciprocally conflicting terms. The operation of the law of *kamma* presupposes both conditionality and changeability. In other words, it is only on account of a person's inherent susceptibility to conditioning that *kamma* will find space to function. Self as an unchanging absolute entity would not meet that requirement and is therefore irrelevant as far as the law of *kamma* is concerned. In this way, the doctrine of nonself further substantiates the law of *kamma* and makes it more acceptable to the critically-minded intellectual.

The conception of soul or self originates from a lack of understanding of the true nature of mind. To rudimentary logic, it seems that there must be an everlasting entity within which thinks, feels, perceives, and makes decisions. Self, according to the common view, is the thinker of thoughts, feeler of sensations, perceiver of perceptions, and maker of decisions. Self is that which is punished and rewarded by the will of the so-called supreme God. Thus is man forever in fear and dread of the Almighty he himself has created.

Buddhist philosophy requires no such imaginary entity. All physio-psychological phenomena are in a state of flux, arising and falling, according to the physical or psychological conditions present at the moment. What is conveniently called 'thinker' is nothing but the thought itself, which keeps rising and falling like all other realities. This is true of sensations, perceptions, and all other mental activities. There is no thinker behind the thoughts, no feeler behind sensations, no perceiver behind perceptions, no decision maker behind the process of making decisions. All these mental activities keep flowing from one moment to another in an intricately interwoven relationship, giving a false notion of permanent self to the unenlightened mind. As *kamma* is itself part of the mind stream, there is no need at all to introduce the concept of self as an agent of the action or a recipient of the result thereof.

## PRACTICAL OBJECTIVES OF THE DOCTRINE OF KAMMA

As *kamma* directly concerns what we do and how we do it, belief in the doctrine of *kamma* can be of great help in the way we conduct ourselves and interact with others, as well as in our spiritual endeavor. The teachings enable us to establish a clear moral understanding based on reason and the principle of cause and effect. With confidence in the law of *kamma*, one develops a more realistic and rational attitude toward life and its experiences and is inspired to rely on one's ability to fulfill one's own aspirations rather than resort to prayer for extraneous assistance and support.

The law of *kamma* helps us to be more convinced of our own potential and responsibilities, both personal and social, and encourages us to do what is good and to refrain from what is evil or unwholesome. It teaches us to cultivate responsibility toward oneself by giving up bad habits and actions, and responsibility toward others by showing them kindness and compassion. *Kamma* demonstrates that each and every one of us is endowed with potential for greater development and it is within our reach to create a better world, full of love and joy, or to destroy it with hatred and war. We have the choice before us. Understanding *kamma* helps us to make the right choice.

*Kamma* truly puts us in control of our life. We can deal with our present aspirations and plans, and direct future courses of action for our own good as well as for the good of others. This means that we are our own masters and are therefore under an obligation to act with utmost care and responsibility.

Because, according to the doctrine of *kamma*, people should be judged by their actions, not by social status, caste, or creed, the teachings on *kamma* have contributed to the establishment of a universal ethical standard in which moral integrity becomes the norm and the measurement of a person's worth. *Kamma* is that "which classifies beings into coarse and refined states," says the Buddha. He further declares: "Not by birth is one an outcast, not by birth is one a Brahmin. By action is one an outcast, by action is one a Brahmin."

Belief in the doctrine of *kamma* is also essential in the realization of *Nibbāna*. Man must first believe in his own potentialities and the possibility of their cultivation. Spiritual practice means that a person must strongly believe in self-improvement, in removing from his or her mind all that is bad or negative and developing what is positive and good. Without such conviction, spiritual advancement is virtually impossible. Although *Nibbāna* is beyond *kamma*, it is realized through the relinquishment of evil *kamma*, the cultivation of the good, and the purification of mind. Belief in *kamma* may almost be regarded as the be-all and end-all of spiritual discipline.

# 7

# THE FIVE PRECEPTS

## THE PURPOSE OF BUDDHIST MORAL PRECEPTS

THERE ARE THREE FUNDAMENTAL MODES of training in Buddhist practice: morality, mental culture, and wisdom. The English word morality is used to translate the Pali term *sīla*, although the Buddhist term contains its own particular connotations. The word *sīla* denotes a state of normalcy, a condition which is basically unqualified and unadulterated. When one practices *sīla*, one returns to one's own basic goodness, the original state of normalcy, unperturbed and unmodified. Killing a human being, for instance, is not basically human nature; if it were, human beings would have ceased to exist a long time ago. A person commits an act of killing because he or she is blinded by greed, rage or hatred. Such negative qualities as anger, hatred, greed, ill will, and jealousy are factors that alter people's nature and make them into something other than their true self. To practice *sīla* is thus to train in preserving one's true nature, not allowing it to be modified or overpowered by negative forces.

This definition points to the objective of Buddhist morality rather than to the practice itself, but it does give us an idea of the underlying philosophy behind the training, as well as how the Buddhist moral precepts should be followed. These precepts are a means to an end, they are observed for a specific objective.

On the personal level, the observance of precepts serves as the preliminary groundwork for the cultivation of higher virtues or mental development. *Sīla* is the most important step on the spiritual path. Without morality, right concentration cannot be attained, and without right concentration, wisdom cannot be fully perfected. Thus, morality not only enhances people's ethical values and fulfills their noble status as human beings, but it is crucial to their efforts toward the highest religious goal of *Nibbāna*.

On the social level, *sīla* contributes to harmonious and peaceful coexistence among community members and consequently helps to promote social growth and development. In a society where morality prevails and members are conscious of their roles, there will be general security, mutual trust, and close cooperation, these in turn leading to greater progress and prosperity. Without morality there will be corruption and disturbance, and all members of society are adversely affected. Most of the problems that society experiences today are connected, directly or indirectly, with a lack of good morality.

Questions of morality always concern the issues of right and wrong, good and evil. For a moral life to be meaningful these issues must not remain mere theoretical principles, but translated into practice. Good must be performed, evil must be given up. It is not enough to know what is good or evil, we also need to take proper action with respect to them. We need concrete guidelines to follow, and these are provided by the Buddhist moral precepts. Even the oft-quoted Buddhist ideals of abstention from evil, implementation of what is good, and perfect mental purification can be initially actualized through a consistent practice of moral precepts. The precepts help us to live those ideals; they teach us to do the right things and to avoid the wrong.

Buddhist moral precepts provide a wholesome foundation for personal and social growth. They are practical principles for a good life and the cultivation of virtues. If we understand the objectives of *sīla* and realize its benefits, we will see moral precepts as an integral part of life rather than as a burden that we are compelled to shoulder. Buddhist moral precepts are not commandments imposed by force; they are a course of training willingly under-taken in order to achieve a desired objective. We do not practise to please a supreme being, but for our own good and the good of society. As individuals, we need to train in morality to lead a good and noble life. On the social level, we need to help maintain peace and harmony in society and facilitate the progress of the common good. The practice of moral precepts is essential in this regard.

## DISTINGUISHING GOOD AND EVIL

The problems of good and evil, right and wrong, have been dealt with in the discussion on *kamma*. Here it may suffice to give a brief summary on the subject.

To determine whether an action is good or evil, right or wrong, Buddhist ethics takes into account three components involved in a karmic action. The first is the intention that motivates the action, the second is the effect the doer experiences consequent to the action, and the third is the effect that others experience as a result of that action. If the intention is good, rooted in positive mental qualities such as love, compassion, and wisdom, if the result to the doer is wholesome (for instance, it helps him or her to become more compassionate and unselfish), and if those to whom the action is directed also experience a positive result thereof, then that action is good, wholesome, or skillful (*kusala*). If, on the other hand, the action is rooted in negative mental qualities such as hatred and selfishness, if the outcome experi-enced by the doer is negative and unpleasant, and if the recipients of the action also experience undesirable effects from the action or become more hateful and selfish, then that action is unwholesome or unskillful (*akusala*).

It is quite probable that on the empirical level an action may appear to be a mixture of good and bad elements, in spite of the intention and the way it is performed. Thus, an action committed with the best of intentions may not bring the desired result for either the doer or the recipient. Sometimes an action based on negative intentions may produce seemingly positive results (as stealing can produce wealth). Due to lack of knowledge and understanding, people may confuse one set of actions with an unrelated set of results and make wrong conclusions, or simply misjudge them on account of social values and conventions. This can lead to misconceptions about the law of *kamma* and loss of moral consciousness. This is why precepts are necessary in the practice of moral discipline: they provide definite guidelines and help to avoid some of the confusion that empirical observation and social conventions may entail.

Buddhist moral precepts are based on the Dhamma, and they reflect such eternal values as compassion, respect, self-restraint, honesty, and wisdom. These are values that are cherished by all civilizations, and their significance is universally recognized. Moral precepts that are based on such values or directed toward their realization will always be relevant to human society, no matter to what extent it has developed. Moreover, their validity can be empirically tested on the basis of one's own sensitivity and conscience, which are beyond factors of time and place. Killing, for instance, is objectionable when considered from the perspective of oneself being the victim of the action (although when other lives are subjected to the same act, its undesirability may not be felt as strongly). The same is true with regard to stealing, lying, and sexual misconduct. Because Buddhist moral precepts are grounded on these factors, their practicality remains intact even today, and their usefulness is beyond question.

## Precepts for Lay Buddhists

Observance of the five precepts constitutes the minimum moral obligation of a practising lay Buddhist. These five precepts enjoin against killing living beings, taking what is not given (or stealing), sexual misconduct, false speech, and use of intoxicating drink or drugs.

The practice of Buddhist moral precepts deeply affects one's personal and social life. The fact that they represent a course of training which one willingly undertakes rather than a set of commandments wilfully imposed by a God or supreme being is likely to have a positive bearing upon one's conscience and awareness. On the personal level, the precepts help one to lead a moral life and to advance further on the spiritual path. Moreover, popular Buddhism believes that the practice of morality contributes to the accumulation of merits that both support one in the present life and ensure happiness and prosperity in the next. On the social level, observing the five precepts helps to promote peaceful coexistence, mutual trust, a cooperative spirit, and general peace and harmony in society. It also helps to maintain an atmosphere which is conducive to social progress and development, as we can see from the practical implications of each precept.

The first precept admonishes against the destruction of life. This is based on the principle of goodwill and respect for the right to life of all living beings. By observing this precept one learns to cultivate loving kindness and compassion. One sees others' suffering as one's own and endeavors to do what one can to help alleviate their problems. Personally, one cultivates love and compassion; socially, one develops an altruistic spirit for the welfare of others.

The second precept, not to take things which are not given, signifies respect for others' rights to possess wealth and property.

Observing the second precept, one refrains from earning one's livelihood through wrongful means, such as by stealing or cheating. This precept also implies the cultivation of generosity, which on a personal level helps to free one from attachment and selfishness, and on a social level contributes to friendly cooperation in the community.

The third precept, not to indulge in sexual misconduct, includes rape, adultery, sexual promiscuity, paraphilia, and all forms of sexual aberration. This precept teaches one to respect one's own spouse as well as those of others, and encourages the practice of self-restraint, which is of utmost importance in spiritual training. It is also interpreted by some scholars to mean the abstention from misuse of senses and includes, by extension, non-transgression on things that are dear to others, or abstention from intentionally hurting other's feelings. For example, a young boy may practise this particular precept by refraining from intentionally damaging his sister's dolls. If he does, he may be said to have committed a breach of morality. This precept is intended to instill in us a degree of self-restraint and a sense of social propriety, with particular emphasis on sexuality and sexual behavior.

The fourth precept, not to tell lies or resort to falsehood, is an important factor in social life and dealings. It concerns respect for truth. A respect for truth is a strong deterrent to inclinations or temptation to commit wrongful actions, while disregard for the same will only serve to encourage evil deeds. The Buddha has said: "There are few evil deeds that a liar is incapable of committing." The practice of the fourth precept, therefore, helps to preserve one's credibility, trustworthiness, and honor.

The last of the five Buddhist moral precepts enjoins against the use of intoxicants. On the personal level, abstention from intoxicants helps to maintain sobriety and a sense of responsibility. Socially, it helps to prevent accidents, such as car accidents, that can easily take place under the influence of intoxicating drink or drugs. Many crimes in society are committed under the influence of these harmful substances. The negative effects they have on spiritual practice are too obvious to require any explanation.

## THE FIVE PRECEPTS

Theravada Buddhism preserves the Buddha's teachings and conducts religious ceremonies mainly in the original Pali language. The five precepts are also recited in Pali, and their meanings are generally known to most Buddhists. In the following the original Pali text is given in italics, and the corresponding English translation is given side by side:

1.) *Pāṇātipātā veramaṇī sikkhāpadaṁ samādiyāmi:* I observe the precept of abstaining from the destruction of life.

2.) *Adinnādānā veramaṇī sikkhāpadaṁ samādiyāmi:* I observe the precept of abstaining from taking that which is not given.

3.) *Kāmesu micchācārā veramaṇī sikkhāpadaṁ samādiyāmi:* I observe the precept of abstaining from sexual misconduct.

4.) *Musāvādā veramaṇī sikkhāpadaṁ samādiyāmi:* I observe the precept of abstaining from falsehood.

5.) *Surāmerayamajjapamādaṭṭhānā veramaṇī sikkhāpadaṁ samādiyāmi:* I observe the precept of abstaining from intoxicants that cloud the mind and cause carelessness.

The refrain "I observe the precept of abstaining from..." which begins every precept clearly shows that these are not commandments. They are, indeed, moral codes of conduct that lay Buddhists willingly undertake out of clear understanding and conviction that they are good for both themselves and for society.

## PRACTICAL APPLICATION OF THE FIVE PRECEPTS

Training is based on the axiomatic assumption that human beings have the potential for development. In order that this development may be realized, a concrete standard is needed by which people may train themselves. The five precepts are meant to fulfill this need. For example, compassion is a spiritual quality that we all possess to some degree. However, without a conscious and persistent effort to develop it, this important quality may remain rudimentary and weak. By consciously practising the first precept, we bring this compassion to a higher level of development and come a step closer to the realization of the Dhamma. In the process, our conduct becomes more refined and our mind becomes more sensitive to the problems and suffering of others. By practising the second precept we not only purify our livelihood but train in generosity and non-attachment. The third precept has a direct connection with the training in sense restraint, which is an essential feature in higher spiritual development. In fact, enlightenment is not possible without mastery over the senses. The fourth precept deals with training in truthfulness and virtuous speech. The objective of this precept is not only the cultivation of respect for truth, but a way of life that is sincere and free from falsehood in every respect. Even the fifth precept, which enjoins against the use of intoxicants, is not merely negative, for the resultant effects that take place in the mind in terms of mental strength and moral integrity are very positive. The observance of this precept is also a natural precursor to the cultivation of mindfulness and wisdom, which are the essence of insight meditation. Each and every precept increases our awareness of how we may skillfully conduct ourselves in body and speech and helps us to see more clearly whether we are improving in this process of self-discipline.

We may summarize the five precepts in relation to the spiritual qualities that they are likely to produce and promote as follows:

The first precept helps to promote goodwill, compassion, and kindness. The second can be instrumental in developing generosity, service, altruism, non-attachment, contentment, honesty, and right livelihood. The third precept helps to cultivate self-restraint, mastery over the emotions and senses, renunciation, and control of sensual desire. The fourth precept leads to the development of honesty, reliability, and moral integrity. The fifth precept helps to promote mindfulness, clarity of mind, and wisdom.

Self-reliance and responsibility are important features of the practice of Buddhist morality. Because these precepts are meant to be a course of training, it can hardly be expected that each and every practitioner will be able to follow them without committing the slightest error, any more than it can be expected of a music student not to make a single mistake in the course of his lessons. For people with certain temperaments or occupations, some precepts may appear more difficult to follow than the rest, but that should not be an obstacle to making an attempt to keep the precepts. If one is discouraged from practising, one need simply consider that these precepts are a course of training; and training, by definition, implies imperfection and a gradual process of development.

However, for those who are new to Buddhism, it may be a good idea to begin with greater emphasis on those precepts that are easier to follow, bearing the others in mind for later development. For instance, the second and the third precepts obviously need to be practised by virtue of necessity, for they are supported by laws and are in perfect harmony with customs and conventions in all civilized societies. There is, therefore, hardly an excuse for not practising them. Having dealt with these two precepts in this way, the remaining three present much lighter and less daunting a task. In fact, if we understand the contents and meaning of the five precepts correctly, we may come to feel that it is more natural to observe them than not to.

## MORAL PRECEPTS AND LIVELIHOOD

It is not true to say that fishermen, farmers, or hunters cannot observe the first precept. Like people in other trades and occupations, they may not be able to observe all the precepts all the time or in all circumstances, given their family obligations and livelihood, but they can certainly practise them on special occasions, like holy days, or when they are not actually engaged in their professions. In fact, there may be more opportunities to practise than at first seems possible. We observe the precepts in accordance with our abilities, training by degrees until we are able to make the precepts part and parcel of our lives.

In the time of the Buddha there were people engaged in occupations that involved killing, such as hunters or fishermen. Farmers, too, were not free from killing, although the intention involved might not be as direct. For all of these people the precepts were there to be practised, and some were better able to do so than others. Each person has the opportunity to practise to the best of his or her abilities until they become more mature and are spiritually ready to give up occupations or trades that involve unwholesome *kamma*.

One difficulty for some people is the use of alcoholic drinks: some feel discouraged from keeping the fifth precept because some of their friends drink or because they have business dealings with people who drink. Peer pressure and business objectives may be an obstacle to the observance of this precept, but this is by no means insurmountable. Most people are reasonable and do understand religious conscience. Sometimes, citing physicians' opinions may add weight to an excuse not to drink, but it is always best to be honest. In any case, a serious Dhamma practitioner should not allow trivial things like this to prevent him or her from trying to keep the precepts. There is always an opportunity to exert oneself if one is earnest in the practice.

If one carefully studies the foregoing discussion on the five precepts, one will see that, although the Pali texts are worded in the negative "...abstaining from...", there is the positive commitment "I undertake to observe the precept..." in all of them. Negative expressions do not necessarily represent negative or passive attitudes of mind. Of course, misunderstandings may result from misinterpretations of the Buddhist moral precepts (as they arise in regard to other Pali technical terms like *Nibbāna*, *dukkha*, *santutthi*, and *anattā*).

From the practical perspective Buddhist moral precepts do contain both positive and negative aspects. However, from the psychological point of view it is important for practitioners to first recognize that which is bad or wrong and which should be abstained from. Abstention from wrong or evil deeds is the most significant step toward real development in spirituality. Strangely enough, it often appears that people are so preoccupied with doing good, they forget the most important duty of refraining from evil. That is why even though one scientific accomplishment after another is being achieved, crime rates are soaring unchecked, and thinking people begin to question the benefits of those accomplishments. In religious circles, devotees passionately try to accumulate more and more merits without ever pausing to reflect whether there are things that should be cleansed from their minds. As long as this negative aspect is not attended to on a practical level, spiritual progress will not come about. On the other hand, consider a society in which people were determined not to do evil and who abstained from that which is bad and wrong; the result of such a 'negative' practice would indeed be most welcome. Even *Nibbāna* is often negatively described as "the abandoning and destruction of desire and craving," and "the extinction of desire, the extinction of hatred, and the extinction of delusion," although it is positively the highest good.

Once wrong and evil deeds have been abandoned, it becomes more natural to do good. Since life means movement and action, any human expression which rejects evil is bound to be good and positive. If false speech is given up, whatever is spoken will naturally be truthful. Giving up of falsehood, which is a negative act, therefore constitutes in itself not only a negation, but a positive attitude and commitment. As the Buddha himself has admonished his followers:

> "Abandoning false speech, one speaks the truth, becomes dependable, trustworthy, and reliable, and does not mislead the world. Abandoning malicious speech, one does not repeat there what has been heard here, nor does one repeat here what has been heard there, in order to sow the seeds of discord. One reconciles and unites those disunited and promotes closer bonds among friends. Unity is one's delight and joy, unity is one's love, it is the motive behind one's verbal expression. Abandoning harsh speech, one employs a speech which is blameless, pleasant, acceptable, soul-touching, civilized, and agreeable. Abandoning frivolous speech, one uses speech which is appropriate to the occasion, correct, purposeful, and in accordance with the Dhamma-Vinaya. One utters words that are worthy, opportune, reasonable, meaningful, and straightforward."

One important reason why the Buddhist moral precepts are phrased in negative terms is because the negative mode of expression tends to convey clearer and more specific injunctions which can be followed with ease. From a practical point of view, "Do not kill" carries stronger impact and a clearer definition than "Be kind to animals" and can be more conveniently practised. From experience, however, we will see that anyone who consciously and constantly observes the first precept will naturally develop kindness toward people and animals. The second precept, which says, "Do not take what is not given," covers all forms of wrong livelihood, whether by deception, fraud, bribery or theft. By earnestly observing this precept, one will naturally take a positive step in earning one's livelihood in a righteous way. Through constant awareness and direct control of greed and avarice, which motivate wrong livelihood, one learns to develop generosity, altruism, and selfless service. These and other positive virtues result from the so-called negative actions of observing the moral precepts, clearly demonstrating how the precepts laid down by the Buddha can bear positive results, despite their wording and expression.

## MORAL DILEMMAS

The first of the five Buddhist moral precepts is based on the altruistic concept of universal love and compassion. It is not only a way of life and an exercise in personal morality, but also a part of the much larger scheme in spiritual discipline of which purity of body, speech, and mind are indispensable ingredients. As such it makes no exception in its practice, given the lofty ideal to which it is designed to lead. However, in real life situations, we may need a more practical attitude of mind to approach the problem in a more realistic manner.

First of all, we must recognize the fact that destruction of life is a negative act and the volition involved is an unwholesome one. By being honest with ourselves and by impartially contemplating the results that such acts bring, we can realize the wisdom of the first precept and consequently try to abstain from killing in any form. Perfection in the practice comes with spiritual maturity, and until perfection is attained, one needs to be aware of possible imperfections in the practice and try to improve oneself accordingly.

Because perfection in morality requires considerable effort and training, few can achieve it in the beginning. One need not, therefore, feel discouraged, but should learn how progress in the practice can be made through a systematized and graduated process of training. For instance, one may begin by resolving to abandon any killing that is not absolutely necessary. There are people who find pleasure in destroying other creatures, such as those who fish or hunt for sport. This type of killing is quite unnecessary and only demonstrates callousness. Others are engaged in sports which involve pain and suffering to animals and may even cost their lives, such as bull fights, cock fights, and fish fights—all senseless practices designed to satisfy sadistic impulses. One who wishes to train in the Dhamma should avoid having anything to do with this kind of entertainment. One may also resolve to show kindness to other people and animals in an objective and concrete way whenever it is possible to do so. While circumstances may prevent absolute abstention from killing, this may help to refine the mind and develop more sensitivity to the suffering of other beings. Trying to look for an alternative livelihood that does not involve destruction of life is a further step to be considered.

Keeping one's home free of pests or bugs by not creating conditions for their infestation helps reduce the necessity for exterminating them. Ecologically, this is a very commendable practice, since the adverse effects of chemical insecticides on the environment are well known. Prevention is, indeed, better than cure even concerning bugs and beetles. Cleanliness of habitat makes killing in such cases unnecessary. Even in the field of agriculture, insecticide-free farming is becoming increasingly popular and commercially competitive. If people are so inclined and compassion prevails, killing can be greatly avoided even in the real life situations of an ordinary householder with full family obligations and concerns.

In the unlikely event that killing is absolutely inevitable, it may be advisable to note the obvious distinction between killing out of cruelty and killing out of necessity. A person who goes out fishing for pleasure is cruel. While he may love children or make big donations for charitable institutions, as far as spirituality is concerned his mind is not refined enough to be sensitive to the pain and suffering of the poor creatures living in the river. A man who hunts for a living does so because it is necessary to maintain himself and his family. It would seem quite understandable that in the latter case the unwholesome effects would likely be much lighter than the former. The same thing is true in the case of killing for self defense. Killing dangerous animals, vermin, and insects accrues less kammically unwholesome consequences than killing a human being or an animal that serves man (such as a horse, a dog, or an elephant).

## Buddhism, capital punishment and war

As a student of Buddhism, one may realize that each person practices Dhamma according to his or her ability and the opportunities that arise. A policeman on duty patrolling a crime-infested street or a soldier at a border outpost surveying suspicious movements inside hostile territory will experience totally different circumstances in spiritual endeavor from a monk sitting peacefully in his cloistered cell. Yet, what they do have in common is the opportunity to perform their duty. Each must therefore understand how the Dhamma can be best practised, given the situation he is in. All of us are bounded up with certain duties, one way or another. Where policemen and soldiers are concerned, it would be naive to deny that their duties do include the possibility of killing.

It cannot be overemphasized, however, that destruction of life is, from a Buddhist standpoint, never justified. But in discussing the issue under question it is hardly appropriate not to distinguish between spiritual objectives and those of national security and administration. Capital punishment, for instance, is an instrument by which law and order may be effectively maintained for the common good of society, although Buddhism would not advocate that such a measure is conducive to the police officers' spiritual

147

well-being. The principles and purposes on which the police and military institutions were established are as far apart from those on which Buddhist spiritual training was formulated as anything can be. Yet, Buddhism and those secular institutions do coexist now, as they did during the time of the Buddha. Important military chiefs and dignitaries are known to have been the Buddha's most devout followers. One does not, therefore, make the mistake of concluding that a person cannot be a Buddhist, or keep the Buddhist moral precepts for that matter, if he serves in the armed forces or police establishment. As has been said before there are more opportunities to practise the precepts than not to practise; this is true even where the above-mentioned professions are concerned.

### Stealing from the rich to feed the poor

Helping the poor is a commendable effort, but stealing from the rich to fulfill that commitment can hardly be justified. If this were made into a standard practice, society would be in turmoil. Rights of possession would be ignored, and stealing would become the accepted norm. Finally, the practice would defeat itself, and thievery would be recognized as a charitable act. This is hardly a desirable state of affairs; it is something not even remotely resembling a moral condition.

One of the distinct features of the Buddhist moral precepts is the universal character in which they may be practised with benefit by all members of society. For instance, non-stealing (second precept) can be universally observed with desirable results, and the practice will help to promote coexistence, peace, and harmony in society. If this precept were reversed and stealing were made a moral principle, we can immediately see that there would be so much conflict and confusion that society would eventually cease to function. Thus, stealing can never be made a moral act, no matter how ideal and noble the motivation.

## Extramarital sex

This is a rather complex issue involving ramifications in emotional, social, and moral fields. The problem is a cause for concern in modern times, especially in the West where materialism has for so long been the philosophy of life.

The third moral precept advises against all forms of sexual misconduct, which include rape, adultery, promiscuity, paraphilia, and sexual perversions. Actually, the Buddhist commentary emphasizes adultery more than anything else, but if we take into account the purpose and intention of the precept, it is clear that the precept is intended to cover all improper behavior with regard to sex. The broadest interpretation even purports to mean abstention from the misuse of the senses. The expression "misuse of the senses" is somewhat vague. It could refer to any morally unwholesome action committed under the influence of sensual desire or to the inability to control one's own senses. In any case there is no doubt that the third precept aims at promoting, among other things, proper sexual behavior and a sense of social decency in a human civilization where monogamy is commonly practised and self-restraint is a cherished moral value.

For one reason or another, many young people in love are not able to enter into married life as early as they wish. While marriage is still some distance in the future, or even an uncertain quantity, these people enter into relationships, of which sex forms a significant part. This happens not only among adults, who must legally answer to their own conduct, but also among teenagers who are still immature, emotionally unstable, and tend to act in irresponsible ways. Peer pressure and altered moral values are an important contributing factor to the escalation of the problem. The trend toward extramarital sex has become so common that it is now virtually taken for granted. Contubernal arrangements are becoming increasingly popular, and marriage is relegated to a place of insignificance, jeopardizing in the process the sanctity of family life.

In the context of these developments, the third precept becomes all the more relevant and meaningful. Unlike killing, which certain circumstances seem to warrant, there is hardly any plausible excuse for sexual promiscuity, except human weaknesses and inability to restrain the sexual urge. However, there is a distinction between sexual promiscuity and sexual relationship based on mutual trust and commitment, even if the latter were a relationship between two single adults. Thus one may begin to practise the third precept by resolving not to be involved in sexual activities without an earnest intention and serious commitment of both parties. This means that sex should not be consummated merely for the sake of sexuality, but should be performed with full understanding within the people involved and with mutual responsibility for its consequences. A certain level of maturity and emotional stability is necessary to ensure a healthy and productive sexual relationship between two partners. With the realization that there is a better and more noble path to follow than promiscuity, one may see the wisdom of self-restraint and the benefit of establishing a more lasting and meaningful relationship which, rather than impeding one's spiritual progress, may enhance it.

Finally, if anything else fails to convince people of the danger and undesirability of sexual promiscuity, perhaps the phenomenal AIDS epidemic will. This may seem beside the point, since moral precepts and moral integrity are matters that concern inner strength, fortitude, and conscientious practice, not fear and trepidation based on extraneous factors. It is, nevertheless, worthwhile to consider the connection between promiscuous behavior and the AIDS epidemic and realize how strict observance of the third Buddhist moral precept could greatly reduce the risk of infection or spread of this deadly disease. Acceptance of this fact may also lead to an appreciation of the value of morality and moral precepts as laid down by the Buddha, consequently strengthening conviction in the Dhamma practice.

## White lies

The practice of the fourth precept aims at inculcating a respect for truth in the mind, implying both one's own obligations as well as the rights of other people to truth. This is one of the most important components in developing sound social relationships, and it makes all documents, contracts, agreements, deeds, and business dealings meaningful. When we resort to falsehood, we not only become dishonest but also show disrespect to the truth. People who tell lies discredit themselves and become untrustworthy.

It is true that sometimes telling lies may prove more profitable than truth, especially from the material point of view. Because such gains are unwholesome and may cause harm in the long run, and because material profits are likely to lead to more falsehood and fabrication, it is imperative that the practice of the fourth precept be duly emphasized. Where a person's reputation and feelings are concerned, discretion should be exercised. Of course, there are instances where silence is more appropriate than speech, and one may choose this as an alternative to prevarication and falsehood.

Motivation is an important element in determining if one is transgressing the fourth precept and whether a given verbal expression constitutes a kammically unwholesome act. For instance, when an event is fictionalized for literary purposes, this may not be regarded as falsehood as such for the intention of the work is obvious and there is no attempt at falsification involved. Another example is the case of an invective, where an abusive expression is used (such as angrily calling someone a dog). This is a case of vituperation rather than fabrication or falsification, although it is, nonetheless, a kammically unwholesome act. Also, there is a clear distinction between expressing untruth with a selfish intention and with a well-meaning motive, as when a concocted story is told for instructional purposes or a white lie is

151

told in order to keep an innocent child out of danger.

These latter two instances are even accepted as illustrations of the employment of skillful means. A story is told of a mother who returns home to find her house on fire. Her little son is playing in the house, unaware that its burning roof could collapse at any moment. He is so engrossed that he pays no attention to his mother, who is now in great distress, being unable to get into the house herself. So she calls out to her child, "Come quickly, my little one, I have some wonderful toys for you. All the toys you ever wanted to have are here!" In this instance the mother is using a skillful means that eventually saves the boy's life. Under certain circumstances, this may be the only alternative, but indiscriminate use of such means may lead to undesirable results. One needs to be judicious, therefore, in the practice of the precepts.

Sometimes speaking the truth may cause more harm than good, especially if it is done with malicious intent. A vindictive neighbor who spreads the scandals about the family next door may be speaking the truth, but she is neither doing anyone a service, nor is she practising the Dhamma. A spy who sells his nation's sensitive classified information to an enemy may be speaking the truth, but he could cause much harm to his nation's security and jeopardize many innocent lives. The Buddha says, therefore, that one should speak the truth which is useful and conducive to the Dhamma, and should avoid that which is useless and is likely to cause unwholesome *kamma* to oneself and others.

### Intoxicants

The fifth precept covers all intoxicants, including narcotics, that alter the state of consciousness and are physiologically addictive. The danger and negative effects of narcotics, such as cocaine and heroin, are too obvious to require any further elaboration. Today they represent a serious health and social problem around the world.

Drinking intoxicants is not part of the Buddhist culture, although it seems to have become a widespread phenomenon in modern society. It is true that alcoholic consumption was prevalent before and during the time of the Buddha, but he never approved of the practice. The fact that something is commonly practised does not necessarily mean that it is good and wholesome. Those who advocate drinking as a factor for promoting friendship forget to take account of the reality that so many friendships have been drowned in those intoxicants. The brawls, strife and unruly behavior that often follow the consumption of alcoholic beverages represent an unequivocal testimony of the ignoble state to which human beings can be reduced to under the influence of intoxicants. Friendship founded on compassion and mutual understanding is much more desirable than that which is based on alcohol. Social drinking may produce a general euphoric atmosphere among drinkers (and probably a nuisance for nondrinkers), but it is never a necessary condition for interpersonal relationship. Often, people use this as an excuse to get drunk. The high rate of car accidents connected with drunk driving should serve as a strong reminder of the danger and undesirability of alcoholic consumption. On the other hand, it may be mentioned in passing that liquor does contain certain medicinal properties and can be used for medical purposes. Such use, if genuine and under qualified supervision, does not entail transgression of the fifth precept and is not considered a morally unwholesome act.

The most obvious danger of intoxicants is the fact that they tend to distort the sensibilities and deprive people of their self-control and powers of judgment. Under alcoholic influences, a person is likely to act rashly and without due consideration or forethought. Otherwise decent people may even commit murder or rape under the influence of alcohol, or cause all kinds of damage (such as fire, accident, and vandalism) to people or property. The Buddha described addiction to intoxicants as one of the six causes of ruin. It brings about six main disadvantages: loss of wealth, quarrels and strife, a poor state of health (liability to diseases), a source of disgrace, shameless and indecent behavior, and weakened intelligence and mental faculties.

## OTHER PRECEPTS

Occasionally, lay Buddhists may take the opportunity to observe the eight precepts as a means of developing higher virtues and self-control. Of course, these can be practised as often as one wishes, but the special occasions on which they are normally observed are the holy days, especially the more important ones, the three month period of rains retreat, and special events connected with one's life. Sometimes, a Buddhist may observe them even as a token of gratitude and respect to a deceased relative or on the occasion of a birth anniversary of a monk he reveres. Four of these eight precepts are identical with the five precepts mentioned above. In order, they are as follows:

1) to abstain from the destruction of life
2) to abstain from stealing or taking what is not given
3) to abstain from sexual intercourse (to practise celibacy)
4) to abstain from falsehood
5) to abstain from alcoholic drinks
6) to abstain from partaking of food from afternoon till the following daybreak
7) to abstain from singing and entertainments, from decorating oneself and use of perfumes
8) to abstain from the use of large and luxurious beds.

# 8

# MEDITATION

## BUDDHIST MEDITATION

THE PALI WORD FOR MEDITATION PRACTICE is *bhāvanā*, which literally means 'development,' 'cultivation,' or 'culture.' Since this practice has to do directly with the mind, the word *bhāvanā* therefore refers specifically to a process of mental culture or mental development. In this respect the English word 'meditation' is a rather poor and inadequate equivalent of the word *bhāvanā*. In employing the term 'meditation' in the Buddhist context, we should be aware of the character and objective of Buddhist practice.

Buddhist meditation is a means to mental development. It deals particularly with the training of the mind, which is the most important composite of the entire human entity. Because mind is the forerunner and prime source of all actions, physical, verbal, or mental, it needs to be properly cultivated and developed. Buddhist meditation is mental development in the real sense of the term *bhāvanā*, for it aims not only at temporary calm and tranquillity of mind, but at purifying the mind of defilements and negative influences, such as sensual desire, lust, hatred, jealousy, envy, worry, ignorance, restlessness, and indolence. It cultivates and brings to perfection such wholesome and positive qualities of mind as confidence, compassion, wisdom, energy, mindfulness, concentration, and penetrative insight. Meditation is also a practice through which the Dhamma can be realized and the transcendent bliss of *Nibbāna* experienced. It is a useful discipline on all levels of experience, from the ordinary worldly concerns of day-to-day activities up to the highest realization and transcendent spiritual attainment.

Meditation is essentially an experiential activity, not a scholastic subject to be understood through books or secondhand information. It is not an escape from life or evasion from responsibility. Even if the formal meditation practice may appear to the uninformed to be disconnected from real life, its inherent purpose deeply concerns our day-to-day existence and experience. Meditation means mindfulness and wisdom in what we do, speak, and think; it means greater awareness and higher ability in self-control. It is not, therefore, an irrelevant other-worldly practice meant only for monks and ascetics, but is one of the most valuable practical skills there are for enhancing fulfillment in everyday life.

## TYPES OF MEDITATION

Buddhism teaches various methods of meditation practice, but all may be grouped under the two main categories of *samatha* and *vipassanā*. The former refers to concentration (*samādhi*) and is a mode of training designed for the specific purpose of cultivating one-pointedness of mind (*cittekaggatā*); the latter refers to insight, the penetrative mental faculty which perceives and understands realities the way they really are.

Concentration meditation is designed to produce peace and tranquillity of mind (*cittaviveka*) and stronger powers of will, which can be utilized for practical purposes in daily life. Through constant effort and perseverance the meditator may also be able to attain the higher mystic states called *absorption* (*jhāna*). There are eight stages of meditative absorption; the first four are the absorptions of form (*rūpajhāna*), and the remaining ones are formless absorptions (*arūpajhāna*), the highest of which is known as the Sphere of Neither-Perception-Nor-Non-Perception (*nevasaññā-nāsaññā-yatana*). However, all these mystic states are created and conditioned by the mind. They are impermanent and still within the sphere of mundane realities.

Concentration meditation was known prior to the establishment of Buddhism, but it was refined and standardized in the Buddhist system of practice. Nevertheless, in itself it does not lead to the extinction of *dukkha* and the realization of *Nibbāna*, although it may be useful to a certain extent in mental development. Before enlightenment, the Buddha himself practised concentration under some highly accomplished teachers of the day, attaining to the very final stage of absorption, the Sphere of Neither-Perception-Nor-Non-Perception, but he soon discovered that it was unsatisfactory and inadequate as a means for achieving the highest spiritual realization. Concentration can be instrumental for a happy life in this existence (*diṭṭhadhamma-sukhavihāra*), but it is insight meditation that really enables one to purify the mind and realize *Nibbāna*.

Insight meditation is essentially a Buddhist contribution to the spiritual wealth of the world. This is a method of analysis in which the emphasis is placed on the development of mindfulness and knowledge of reality. By applying constant awareness to the present reality of existence, the meditator becomes perfectly identified with his own being and experience. He comes to perceive the realities of impermanence, change, unsatisfactoriness, and non-substantiality in all existential phenomena, and intuitively realizes the true nature of his own inner experiences. All things are characterized by emptiness; in the ultimate analysis there is nothing that should be attached to as 'me' or 'mine.' The meditator sees for himself the wholesome and unwholesome thoughts rising and falling in his mind, the defilements, the virtuous qualities, the good, the evil, the noble, and the ignoble—all are 'seen' and recognized in their true nature. Once the realities are directly intuited and experienced, they can be subjected to further analysis and investigation. Self-knowledge and deeper understanding of realities are obtained through consistent effort and perseverance in the practice of this kind of meditation.

## POPULARITY OF BUDDHIST MEDITATION IN THE WEST

Prof. Donald K. Swearer, a long-time student of Buddhism, observes: "Buddhist meditation is attractive for many reasons, to be sure. For some it offers a retreat from the chaos and complexity of today's world. For others it may serve as a means of introspective self-understanding; and for still others it is the means for attempting seriously to grasp the truth of Buddhism." This statement clearly epitomizes how Buddhist meditation can serve a utilitarian objective for people living in the West and how it may hold immense potential for fulfilling their socio-psychological needs. Westerners are, as a rule, practical and goal-oriented people; they are not satisfied with mere theory, but are more interested in experiencing the results of a given principle. Meditation is a discipline that satisfactorily answers to this type of mentality.

The stressful life-style in Western society may be the strongest reason why people are initially attracted to Buddhist meditation. Excessive materialism, the 'rat race,' and the seeking for all the so-called good things in life have combined to produce a society which is full of stress and tension. The need to compete in order to get to the top is relentlessly driving people forward with no time to pause or slow down. The wastefulness of consumerism represents a serious threat to the world's natural resources and environmental stability; unethical commercialism has produced distrust among manufacturers and consumers. Society seems to be more chaotic than we are officially prepared to admit. In such a context, some people are more inclined to find solace and peace in the dynamic quietude of Buddhist meditation. Through the practice they discover that the most practical way to solve man's problems—personal, social, or global—is to begin with their own minds and attitudes. Buddhist meditation offers a variety of techniques for developing mental clarity and an undistorted view of life, and these are fundamental to the real solution of the problems.

In many cases, Western interest in Buddhist meditation is not solely motivated by problems such as stress or tension, but stems from a genuine conviction in the Dhamma and a curiosity about its practices. This group of practitioners consist mainly of intellectuals and students of Buddhism, who find in the religion something that answers their questions and needs. But no matter what the motivation, earnest meditators always stand to benefit from the practice, and that is one of the most attractive features of Buddhist meditation.

## Practical purpose of Buddhist meditation

Doubts about this topic betray a typical misunderstanding concerning Buddhist meditation, prevalent not only among non-Buddhists but also among certain sectors of Buddhists as well. Some people believe that meditation serves no practical purpose and is an escape from the reality of everyday life. Those who embrace this wrong view fail to distinguish between an active training attuned to a state of perfect mental health, tranquillity, and equilibrium, which is Buddhist meditation, and a passive engagement in nothing but mystic musings or recitation of mantras, which has nothing to do with Buddhist meditation. They also fail to understand that sitting with closed eyes or repeating unintelligible phrases does not in itself constitute Buddhist meditation. Buddhist meditation by no means implies an escape from life. Its practice is largely based on life activities and its effects are meant to improve the quality of life. To develop a high level of concentration a certain degree of seclusion or a carefully-structured environment may be more favorable, but Buddhist meditation means much more than just concentration practice. In fact, the Buddha pointed out that concentration for its own sake is an obstacle to the higher realization of the Dhamma. Nevertheless, the image of a meditating monk sitting cross-legged, still as a rock, and deeply absorbed in meditation, may have created a general wrong impression that it is the only way to practise meditation.

Because meditation, as the original Pali term *bhāvanā*, is the development of the mind, and because mind is the most important determinant by which our physical, verbal, and mental actions are conditioned and controlled, the practice of meditation can bring infinite gains and benefits. The ultimate spiritual benefit attainable through meditation is perfect enlightenment and the realization of *Nibbāna*. However, *Nibbāna* may appear to be too remote a goal for many meditators who simply aspire to more mundane benefits. Listed below are some of the advantages that can be immediately experienced in meditation practice.

1. Meditation increases awareness of inner potentialities and helps us to be more positive in life.

2. Meditation helps to fortify will power and increase self-confidence.

3. Meditation provides mental calm and tranquillity and frees the mind from restlessness, agitation, fear, and worry.

4. Because meditation promotes mental health, it can positively influence physical health. People who are free from worry and mental turmoil, whose minds are calm and serene, usually enjoy comparatively good health.

5. By helping the mind to concentrate and become better organized, meditation can help increase efficiency in day-to-day

work and in the performance of duties and responsibilities.

6. Meditation promotes virtuous qualities like compassion, good will, confidence (*saddhā*), wisdom, energy, perseverance, determination, etc.

7. Meditation helps to purify the mind of defilements (*kilesa*) such as greed, selfishness, hatred, and jealousy, and frees it from the preconceptions and delusions that normally prevent proper insight into reality. A meditator is therefore capable of seeing things the way they really are and can better deal with the life experience.

There are no limits to the benefits that can be derived from the practice of meditation. These benefits can be applied to personal and interpersonal use depending on circumstances and the ability of the meditators themselves. However, it should be added here that the amount of benefit derived from meditation and the measure of success in the practice may be related to such incidental factors as proper understanding of the subject, consistency in the practice, self-confidence, and the degree of perseverance. An experienced teacher can be a great support, especially in the initial stages of training.

## COMPARISON OF SAMATHA AND VIPASSANĀ

*Samatha* means calm or concentration, and *vipassanā bhāvanā* is a mental training process in which mindfulness is the most important element. Although concentration and mindfulness are two distinct mental faculties, having functions of their own, they do depend on one another and should therefore be cultivated together in a balanced manner. In fact, they may be compared to the two ends of the same stick. If you pick up one, the other will come up. In this way the two are inseparable, although functionally they may constitute two separate roles.

The relationship between concentration and mindfulness is

somewhat delicate and sensitive. By definition, concentration refers to the faculty of mind to focus on a single object in a sustained and uninterrupted manner. In order to achieve the state of one-pointedness, it is necessary for the attention to remain unremittingly focused on the meditation object for a long period of time. This presupposes the use of force; the meditator constantly applies his will power to retain mental focus on the object of meditation.

Mindfulness, on the other hand, requires no use of force or will to maintain a mental focus other than the application of bare awareness to the object of experience. Constant practice of mindfulness leads to refined sensibilities and the ability to recognize realities according to their true nature. When developed together with concentration, mindfulness performs the function of selecting an object for concentration and subtly helping to maintain the focus on that particular object. It is a state of bare awareness of the object of experience, involving no desire or aversion, no force of will or attachment.

If mindfulness is strong, it is likely that concentration will become more strengthened, and vice versa. There is the classical analogy of sunlight through a magnifying glass: When sunlight is focused through a magnifying glass, it becomes so concentrated that fire may result. Left to itself, the sun may not be powerful enough to produce that burning effect, although it certainly contains the potential to do so. The lens is therefore instrumental in actualizing the sun's inherent potential. In the same way, the human mind possesses powerful forces and vast potential, which can be harnessed and actualized through the practice of concentration. When the mind is well concentrated, mindfulness is more able to refine the inner sensibilities and to sharpen mental faculties. This finally leads to the development of penetrative insight that enables meditators to perceive all phenomena in their true and undistorted state and to purify their minds of all defilements.

In terms of method and application, mindfulness is broader and more comprehensive than concentration. Mindfulness is inclusive, while concentration is exclusive. Because it is capable of taking all kinds of experiences and phenomena as objects of investigation, mindfulness represents an all-encompassing function. The possibilities of its objects and application are unlimited. Mindfulness is capable of taking in and dealing with everything that comes within the field of sensory and mental experience, leaving nothing aside, while concentration focuses on one single object that has been chosen for the purpose and rejects all others. Basically, it is concentration that generates the mental power and the necessary stillness of mind that mindfulness requires for a deeper penetration into the more profound levels of human consciousness. If concentration is energy, mindfulness provides direction and guidance to that energy. Concentration and mindfulness balanced in proportion will result in greater understanding and insight, which are most vital in spiritual practice.

Right concentration is a wholesome type of one-pointedness which supports wisdom and strengthens other wholesome virtues. Thanks to the power of concentration, mental contaminants such as sensual desire, ill-will, laziness, sloth and torpor, and vacillation, are suppressed, giving an opportunity for wholesome spiritual qualities to arise and grow. If concentration is weakening or the mind drifts from the meditation object, mindfulness immediately takes note of that and assists concentration to regain its footing. It is the function of concentration to stabilize the mind and hold the mental focus steady onto the object of meditation. Mindfulness plays a supportive role and in addition continues on from where concentration ends. In this way, concentration and mindfulness mutually coordinate and depend on each other throughout the whole process of mental culture which is meditation.

## IS MEDITATION SELFISH?

There are a number of points to be considered here. In the first place, meditation cannot be said to be a selfish activity, or meditators self-centered individuals, any more than one may accuse college students who attend college and concentrate on their studies of being selfish in the face of social problems. Meditation is basically a course of training, and one of the most natural outcomes of the practice is the destruction, partly or wholly, of selfishness. Just as going to college equips one with greater ability to be productive and to contribute to society, training in meditation helps one to do good for others with greater sacrifice and dedication. However, while being more educated does not necessarily imply a lesser degree of selfishness, greater spiritual advancement attainable through meditation does. Higher education may even prove to be more socially counterproductive, if excessive greed and selfishness predominate a person's decisions and actions. Meditation, on the other hand, is free from such drawbacks, since what is actually achieved in the course of training is the elimination of negative mental qualities, especially selfishness, and cultivation of the positive ones like compassion, kindness, and wisdom. Far from being selfish, meditation is an entirely virtuous and positive activity.

Secondly, it must be reiterated here that meditation does not necessarily mean sitting cross-legged with closed eyes, reciting a mantra. Those who think that meditation is only a passive engagement with the mind having nothing to do with worldly existence are greatly mistaken. Buddhist meditation deals with life; it is an intensely vital activity. Meditation can be practised while eating, drinking, thinking, gardening, farming, and engaging in other kinds of activities, personal or social. It is therefore improper to say that meditation is a selfish activity. As a matter of fact, nothing is farther from the truth.

Thirdly, meditation is something we live with, not simply a practice for its own sake. The Buddha and his noble disciples are said to have dwelled constantly in meditation, but they were most active in working for happiness and welfare of other people, with no thought or expectation of reward. Their activities produced such great benefit for society and humanity at large because their minds were free of greed, selfishness, ill-will, and other kinds of defilements. People who unduly hasten to engage in social activities without sufficiently preparing their own spiritual groundwork are likely to create more harm than help, and whatever service they manage to render may become little more than an extension of their ego. Examples such as the Crusades, the Salem witchcraft trials, and the Inquisition are not lacking in the history of religions, and they stand as clear testimonies of how dangerous human beings can become if their mental defilements are not properly dealt with. By practising meditation, one becomes aware of one's own mind and thoughts, strengths and weaknesses, and the various subtle manners, including seemingly beneficial social actions, in which egotism may manifest itself.

## IS MEDITATION A KIND OF RUNNING AWAY?

This question demonstrates yet another serious misunderstanding concerning Buddhist meditation. Mental purification is one of the many benefits of meditative practice; it is not the only objective of the discipline. To purify the mind is not to reject existential realities or to run away from them. On the contrary, the process of training requires that meditators learn to recognize realities as they occur from one moment of experience to another. Meditation is, in fact, the most daring kind of practice, one in which one learns to squarely encounter realities; there is no better way to deal with them than through meditation.

The existential realities that we have to contend with are not only external phenomena like earthquakes, flash floods, the AIDS epidemic, child prostitution, or high crime rates. More intimate and closer to ourselves are the inner experiences that we feel and perceive in each and every moment. These experiences are no less real and tangible than other seemingly more concrete events that are happening in other parts of the world. They are the most immediate realities we have to contend with, and if they are not handled properly, chances are that we will add more problems and cause more suffering to ourselves and the world.

Buddhist meditation, especially insight meditation, represents a unique mode of practice by which meditators are trained to recognize realities without bias and fully experience life as it is. We learn to go beyond our inherent preconceptions and illusions, and try to analytically deal with our experiences in an objective manner. This enables us to perceive things as they really are, not as we are conditioned, positively or negatively, to see them. Most importantly, we learn how to see ourselves in a clear, straightforward way, understanding our own character and temperaments, weaknesses and shortcomings. Buddhist meditation is a noble method of accepting reality. It is the most practical way to deal with the realities of life.

## CAN MEDITATION CAUSE INSANITY?

To say that meditation causes insanity is as true as the assertion that eating can cause death or brushing teeth may cause mouth injury. Actually, insanity can be produced in many different ways. Normal activities such as studying in college, business dealings, playing the stock market, and even love affairs, all hold the potential to induce insanity. It really depends on one's attitude of mind and on how these activities are carried out. If you stretch yourself to an extreme by studying all day and night without a rest or working nonstop without going to sleep, then there are good chances of developing mental problems or neuroses. There are also reports of those whose sweet love turns sour and, through the agony of a broken heart, suffer emotional imbalance and insanity. Practically anything can be cited as a potential cause for mental derangement.

Those who assert that meditation can cause insanity do not really understand what Buddhist meditation is and how it is practised. Far from being a cause for mental disorder or the loss of sanity, meditation is rather a subtle art for promoting mental health of the highest order. We have seen that in meditation practice, mindfulness is the most important factor, and it is mindfulness that has to be constantly developed and applied to one's psycho-physical experiences in each and every moment. This leads to the growth of other virtuous qualities such as compassion, generosity, morality, wisdom, energy, perseverance, and selflessness. It is therefore appropriate to assert that meditation is, in fact, not only conducive to emotional stability and psychological well-being, but also greatly contributes to spiritual advancement and enhances personal and social lives.

It is most probable that people whose mental constitutions are abnormal, who are afflicted with a severe case of mental disorder, such as paranoid schizophrenia, may not be ready for meditation practice. These individuals are prone to display uncontrollable and erratic behavior and are likely to suffer some degree of insanity no matter what spiritual discipline they undertake or what activities they may engage in. If they indulge in meditation practice without first taking sufficient professional care of their problems, one would not expect them to fare very well in the training.

There are also those who profess certain ideas about meditation and start an intensive practice on their own. Without proper background knowledge or guidance, it is possible that such practice may result in a loss of mental equilibrium and hallucinations. But meditation cannot be held accountable for these negative effects. Buddhist meditation is completely safe and wholesome when undertaken with the proper frame of mind and under the guidance of a capable teacher.

## MEDITATION TECHNIQUE

Because of lack of space, not all the methods or details of the practice of concentration meditation can be given here. However, we may discuss the most fundamental concepts and techniques of training to give readers a clear understanding of how meditation is undertaken in the initial stages; those who are interested in putting these techniques into practice may do so without harm or adverse effects if moderation is duly observed.

Concentration is developed by single-mindedly focusing the attention on a selected object. There is a wide range of objects that can be used for meditation, and forty have been specifically recommended in Buddhist literature, although it is quite possible that other things may be included in the list as well. Classical examples are one's own breaths, a Buddha image, a candlelight, a painted disc or dyed cloth stretched on a round frame (*kasina*), water, empty space, etc. The reason why a rather large variety of objects is described is to provide a wide choice for practitioners with different preferences and temperaments. A suitable object of meditation facilitates the practice and ensures better progress.

The meditator can, if so desired, initially experiment with different objects of concentration to see which is most suitable. Very often this may not be necessary if one chooses to commence the practice with a more convenient device, like one's own breaths. A good meditation object is one on which the practitioner finds it easier to concentrate. With the help of an experienced teacher, a right decision is made much easier. On one's own, a student of meditation may experiment until satisfied with the choice. However, once the decision has been made, it makes more sense to stick to whatever has been selected rather than keep changing the meditation object, otherwise the practitioner will become confused and the practice will not progress as well as it should.

The concentration technique which involves a prolonged and constant focus on one's own breaths has been praised by the Buddha as being suitable to all types of temperaments. This technique is so popular that it is virtually taught in all Buddhist traditions. It is so convenient to practise that even children, properly instructed, can do it.

There are different ways by which concentration on the breath is developed. In other words, one may say that there are numerous ways and means to use one's breaths as the object of concentration practice. These may be regarded simply as different variations of the same method, and they are so many that it is impossible to list all of them here. Individual meditation centres may have a specific preference for one variation over others, although all are equally valid and beneficial. For the sake of illustration, we may cite the method in which the two-syllable Pali word *bud-dho* is employed as an aid to cultivate concentration. This is how it is done:

Sit cross-legged, placing the right foot on the left. Keep the back straight and upright, but not uncomfortably rigid. If your legs are stiff, being unaccustomed to the cross-legged maneuver, and you find this posture uncomfortable, try using a cushion to support yourself from underneath so that the weight of the body will be less pressing on the legs and your feet enjoy a little more room. If this is still a problem, you may sit on a chair, although this is not a traditional posture. (Most people in Asia can sit cross-legged with ease.) Sitting in the traditional way is said to effect a sense of stability and helps to prepare you for the task of meditation that will follow. In any case you should feel sufficiently comfortable that you do not have to move for a specific period of time during the practice.

Having properly settled down, put your hands on your lap, the right one on the left, palms upward. Close your eyes and begin to relax your body. You may will the different parts of the body to relax, starting from the head downward and working with all the muscles in each part. Do it slowly, in a leisurely manner, and systematically, avoiding nothing in the process. This will take roughly two to three minutes, and by the time you have completed this preparatory stage, your mind should have been appropriately attuned to the meditation practice proper. You should be completely relaxed, otherwise meditation will become more of a burden than the enjoyable spiritual experience that it is. Not only should you feel physically relaxed, you should also train your mind to be free from psychological tension by putting down for the time being any cares and concerns that may cause mental disturbance or restlessness. Careful attention to small details prior to the sitting, like making sure that the door is locked, the gas stove or television set turned off, and the telephone unplugged or moved to another area where it will not be a nuisance, can add much to the pleasure of the practice and further ensure success in the endeavor.

When you have gained a certain amount of relaxation and composure, turn your attention to the in- and out-breaths. Now you become clearly conscious of your own respiration, which has hardly been noticed before. Keep focusing on your in- and out-breaths to the exclusion of anything else until your mind becomes further composed and still. Mentally repeat the syllable *bud* (as in Buddha) as you breathe in and *dho* as you breathe out. Synchronize each syllable of *bud-dho* with the in- and out-breath so that they become completely identified with one another. Keep the body unmoved and the mind still through the time assigned for the practice. In the likely event that your mind gets distracted or starts to roam about, gently bring it back to the object of meditation which is your in- and out-breaths. Continue to do this and your mind will gradually become one with your breaths and attain the state of one-pointedness.

In this technique of concentration practice, inhalation and

exhalation are employed as a tool to keep the mind still and focused. The mental recitation of *bud-dho* serves to fortify the practice. Some meditators may find this a more convenient concept on which to retain their attention. For Buddhists, it adds a distinct flavor of faith to the training, because the Pali word *bud-dho* really signifies the Buddha. Some meditators prefer to use the nose-tip as a point of mental focus; others may like to follow the inhalation movement down from the nostrils to the abdomen and the exhalation movement up from the abdomen through the nostrils, especially if they are newcomers to meditation. The breathing technique is the most popular form of Buddhist meditation; its practicality and usefulness have been universally recognized wherever Buddhism is taught. The incorporation of *bud-dho* into the practice is distinctly a Thai contribution and the technique is very widespread in the country.

## DIFFERENT LEVELS OF CONCENTRATION

Obviously, the strength of concentration differs in different stages of training. The Buddhist commentaries mention three levels of concentration. The first, momentary concentration (*khaṇika samādhi*), is a quality of mind that is inherently common in all sentient beings. This is an essential faculty that we all need in our everyday activities, and we can experience it even when we are engaged in the most mundane chores like eating, drinking, reading, writing a letter, or driving. In fact, it seems impossible to perform any function effectively without a certain amount of concentration. In the same way, it may also be said that our capacity and efficiency to work depend largely on the amount of concentration we are able to mobilize in the fulfillment of our duties. Thus a higher degree of concentration almost invariably means a better performance of actions. However, this type of concentration is hard to control and not very stable. It is momentary. Normally, it is sustained by the interest we pay to objects of sense stimuli at the moment of experience; as soon as the interest weakens, we will also begin to lose concentration and will have to refocus our attention.

The second level, called access or approximate concentration (*upacāra samādhi*), is a more developed form of concentration attainable through the process of mental development mentioned above. At this stage, the mind of the meditator is elevated beyond the ordinary level of consciousness but is not as yet well established in deep concentration. The state of one-pointedness of mind is still subject to some degree of instability and fluctuation, although it can be better controlled than in the first type of concentration. Concentration at this particular level provides the necessary basis for the practice of insight meditation, and one need not develop it further should one chose to develop insight. However, if the meditator prefers to continue with concentration training, this stage will prove an important juncture where his consciousness has reached a higher stratum of spiritual accomplishment and is acutely attuned to attain higher, more steady one-pointedness of mind.

The third level is attainment concentration (*appanā samādhi*). This is a stage where the meditator's mind becomes well established in one-pointedness and is completely under control. This means that at this level the meditator is in a position to retain concentration for as long as he or she wishes, and the concentration reached is so profound and deep it cannot be disturbed by any external elements. It is total mastery over oneself, a mastery that is potentially capable of defying even the known laws of nature. Here the meditator has become so entirely absorbed in the object of meditation that he or she appears to be wholly identified with it. This kind of concentration is the foundation of *jhāna* or absorption. From this level of concentration, the meditator enters into the first absorption, and if one continues to persevere in one's effort, one will progress even further to higher stages of absorption.

# HIGHER BENEFITS OF CONCENTRATION

We have seen from the above discussion that concentration meditation involves force, will power, and mastery of mind. The inner powers generated through a high intensity of concentration may be used to influence other people and events. This is still rudimentary compared to what the higher states of mental development can achieve, and such powers are not the real objective of meditation practice and were not encouraged by the Buddha. Due to the limitations of modern life-styles, few people can afford the luxury of full-time practice as ascetics in mountain caves or forests. However, if one consistently perseveres until attainment concentration (*appanā samādhi*) is gained, one may continue to achieve any of the eight levels of absorption.

The first four (five, according to the Abhidhamma) absorptions result from meditation on some concrete form such as earth, fire, water, or a kasiṇa (colored disc), etc. A state of absorption achieved through the practice in this way is called absorption of form (*rūpajhāna*).

The other four are called absorptions of the formless sphere (*arūpajhāna*) because, rather than focusing the mind on any concrete form, the meditator employs abstract concepts as objects of concentration. These conceptual objects are the sphere of infinity of space (*ākāsānañcāyatana*), the sphere of infinity of consciousness (*viññāṇañcāyatana*), the sphere of nothingness (*ākiñcaññāyatana*), and the sphere of neither perception nor non-perception (*nevasaññānāsaññāyatana*). To practise the absorptions of the formless sphere one has to be first thoroughly accomplished in the four absorptions of form.

Concentration increases the power of mind. This can be brought to such a high level that psychic wonders, or what one may call 'miracles,' can be performed through it, although we should again emphasize that psychic powers or miracles are neither the purpose nor the goal of Buddhist meditation. In fact, the Buddha even laid down rules for the monks against the display of such feats, for they are likely to distract the uninformed and mislead them from the path of enlightenment and deliverance from *Saṁsāra*, which is the true goal of Buddhism. In the Buddhist system of meditation, right concentration is that which serves as the basis for insight. It is a means to an end, not an end in itself.

## PRACTICE OF INSIGHT MEDITATION

This properly requires a long description, but for reasons of space and balance we shall have to limit our discussion only to a brief description of this uniquely Buddhist meditation practice.

For the sake of clarity we may begin by briefly comparing some salient features in the two types of meditation, concentration and insight, which we have been discussing at some length. To practise concentration, a properly structured environment or atmosphere is required. For example, the environment should be relatively secluded and quiet, somewhat segregated from other activities, and completely free from disturbances. Insight meditation does not need any of these requirements, although in the initial stages of practice they may prove valuable. Concentration training employs only one object as a tool for cultivating one-pointedness of mind, whereas insight meditation uses all available experiences as the primary matrix by which mindfulness and insight may be developed. The fact that insight meditation can take in all experiences, physical, emotional, and psychological, as its objects of training also means that one can practise it in all activities and situations. Concentration does not enjoy this kind of free range. So we may assert that insight meditation is one spiritual discipline that can be practised at all times, in all places, and under all circumstances. Concentration and insight are also different in terms of the objectives and goals each aims to achieve. The former is connected with one-pointedness of mind, tranquillity, psychic powers, and miracles, whereas the latter aims at increased awareness, knowledge, wisdom, right understanding, virtues, purification of the mind, and the realization of *Nibbāna*.

One of the most important discourses by the Buddha dealing with insight meditation is the *Satipaṭṭhāna Sutta*, or the Discourse on the Foundations of Mindfulness. This discourse contains what is considered by all Buddhist traditions to be the classical explanation of how insight meditation should be practised. In the opening words of the discourse, the Buddha categorically affirms that the development of mindfulness in accordance with the *Satipaṭṭhāna Sutta* constitutes the direct way, the only way, to purification, the extinction of suffering, and the realization of *Nibbāna*. It is one of the few discourses in which the Buddha has so explicitly and unequivocally given such a strong assurance.

According to the *Satipaṭṭhāna Sutta*, mindfulness is the key factor in the development of insight. This mindfulness is the quality of awareness which is applied to four groups of experiences, namely, the body, the sensations, the mind, and mental objects (particularly in reference to moral and spiritual experiences or the Dhamma). Thus the discourse is divided into four principal sections, each dealing with an individual class of experiences on which mindfulness should be cultivated.

The first of the Four Foundations of Mindfulness deals with the body (*kāya*). This includes the breaths, the physical postures, the bodily activities, the analysis of various physical components, the material elements, and death. These are the realities of life one has to deal with. A student of insight meditation should practise by constantly applying mindfulness to all these experiences founded on the body. For instance, he should be attentively mindful of his breaths, noting their ever-changing characteristics to see if they are short or long, shallow or deep, refined or gross, regular or irregular, and so forth. The purpose is to train the mind to dwell in the present, by being constantly aware of what goes on at the moment. The same principle may be applied to the bodily posture, such as standing, walking, sitting, or lying down, as well as to other physical activities like eating and drinking, or even the movements of feet and hands. In the words of the Buddha:

> "Monks, a monk should further apply full attention to the act of going forward or going back, looking straight or looking away, bending or stretching, putting on his robes or holding the bowl, eating, drinking, chewing or savoring food, attending to the calls of nature, walking, standing, sitting, falling asleep, waking up, speaking, or being silent. In all these activities he should be fully aware and attentive."

The second section deals with feelings (*vedanā*), which are of three types, pleasant, unpleasant, and neutral. These feelings keep arising one after the other and the meditator should apply mindfulness to them at the moment they arise, understanding them objectively as conditioned phenomena that arise and fall according to the law of causality, not subjectively as 'my feeling.'

Sensations or feelings have a peculiar way of misleading us into a false sense of individuality. Because of feelings, man tends to conceptualize an essential agent within that feels or does the act of feeling, the recipient of various experiences, including the results of *kamma*. This is called a soul or self. According to the Buddha, the false belief in the existence of self is largely due to our feelings. It is therefore important that the meditator trains himself to perceive reality as it is by simply observing his own feelings for what they really are, natural phenomena that constantly arise and disappear in accordance with their conditionality.

Another way to consider feelings is the careful analysis of their nature and their origination and dissolution. The meditator is fully mindful whether he experiences pleasant, unpleasant, or neutral feeling. He is aware of the feelings but does not become attached to them. Says the Buddha:

> "Here, a meditating monk dwells observing feelings internally,

externally, or internally and externally. He dwells observing the nature of origination, dissolution, or origination and dissolution of feelings. His mindfulness is established merely to an extent necessary for knowledge and awareness that feelings exist. He lives unattached and clings to nothing in the world. In this way a monk dwells observing feelings."

The next section in the discourse deals with the mind. If part of the spiritual practice involves the ability to understand and control one's own thoughts, this is, perhaps, one of the most effective methods to realize that objective. Here, the meditator dwells observing his own mind and thoughts, ever mindful of their origination and dissolution. He also observes how they change and are conditioned. The meditator should constantly apply full awareness to the present moment of experiences only, not the past or the future, and simply acknowledge the existence and nature of those mental phenomena. There is no conscious intervention involved to suppress one thought or encourage another. It is a simple, uncomplicated process of recognizing the realities as they are, a pure psychological act of detached understanding and acceptance.

The *Satipaṭṭhāna Sutta* gives an elaborate explanation of the techniques for observing the mind and recognizing its conditions in the present moment. We quote below some examples from the text:

> "Here a meditating monk recognizes the lustful mind as lustful; the non-lustful mind as non-lustful; the hateful mind as hateful; the non-hateful mind as non-hateful; the deluded mind as deluded; the non-deluded mind as non-deluded; the depressed state of mind as depressed; the distracted state of mind as distracted; the cultivated state of mind as cultivated; the uncultivated state of mind as uncultivated ... "

It is clear from this short passage how a practitioner may train in insight meditation by steadfastly being mindful of his own mental states. By continually practising according to this method, one not only comes to understand oneself better but will eventually be able to penetrate deeply into the most remote reaches of one's own consciousness. Thus one learns to come to terms with oneself, and a genuine effort to improve oneself and do away with weaknesses may now begin. This kind of practice is not only valuable as far as insight is concerned, but substantially contributes to peace and harmony, both within the individual and within society. If one, for instance, keeps taking mindful note of one's own greed, lust, anger, or aggression as they arise in the mind, it is most probable that the thoughts or actions associated with such negative qualities will be recognized as quickly as they originate and will subsequently be kept under control or eliminated. It is like having your hitherto clandestine enemies duly exposed so you can take appropriate action against them. There is no better way to deal with them than this.

The last section of the *Satipaṭṭhāna Sutta* discusses the Dhamma as the system of ethical and spiritual experiences. In practical terms, this may also include mindfulness in contemplation, deliberation, and investigation of the Buddha's teachings in the context of one's own perception at the present moment. Because these Dhamma experiences are subjected to the contemplation and investigation of mind, they are referred to as mental objects. A few categories of Dhamma are listed in the *Satipaṭṭhāna Sutta*: the Five Hindrances, the Five Aggregates, the Six Sense Bases, the Seven Factors of Enlightenment, and the Four Noble Truths. Detailed explanations illustrative of the practice are also given, for example:

> "How, monks, does a monk dwell observing the Five Hindrances as mental objects? Here, when sense desire is present, a monk comprehends, "Sense desire is present in me;" when sense desire is not present, he comprehends, "Sense desire is not present in me." He comprehends how non-arisen sense desire arises; he comprehends how arisen sense desire disappears. He comprehends how abandoned sense desire will not arise in the future ..."

Broadly speaking, most of the deliberate intellectual exercises pertaining to ethics and truth come within the scope of this mode of insight meditation. To be more precise, however, each of the aforementioned categories of the Dhamma should not be viewed merely as a subject for academic scrutiny or an article for purely abstract contemplation. Rather, they are specific mental objects to which a meditator should apply mindfulness as and when they are actually experienced and comprehended, right at the moment of their arising and disappearing. In this way the meditator will be able to understand the Dhamma not as some abstract concept, but as the actual reality of personal experience which it truly is.

The Four Foundations of Mindfulness as described by the Buddha can be practised simultaneously, depending on which of the four is more prominent or conspicuous at the moment of experience. The present moment is what counts, not the past or the future.

Beginners may find it more practicable to begin training with mindfulness on the body, particularly the breathing exercises. Once the basic technique has been mastered, it becomes increasingly more natural to 'ever dwell in meditation,' constantly and effortlessly observing the body, the feelings, the mind, and the mental objects while carrying on their duties and responsibilities.

## CONCENTRATION IN INSIGHT MEDITATION

Concentration in *samatha bhāvanā* is characterized by its mundane nature and objective, whereas the same in *vipassanā* is directed toward the transcendent goal of *Nibbāna*. Concentration in insight meditation, moreover, assists the meditator to penetrate into the three existential realities in all experiences to which he applies his mindfulness. These are the characteristics common to all existence, namely, impermanence, unsatisfactoriness, and non-substantiality. Based on these three signs of reality, *vipassanā* concentration is therefore divided into three types as follows:

The first kind of concentration is called *suññatā samādhi*, meaning concentration on the void. This is the concentration which is specifically based on *anattalakkhaṇa* or the characteristic of soullessness. It supports and identifies with the insight that contemplates on the relative, non-substantial nature of realities. This insight aims primarily at liberation through penetration into the soulless nature of all things.

The second category of *vipassanā* concentration is known as *animittasamādhi*. Animitta means "signless," an expression referring to the transitoriness of existence. This concentration supports insight which contemplates the impermanent nature of all things (*aniccalakkhaṇa*), particularly the experiences to which the meditator's awareness is applied in the training of insight meditation. Here, liberation is achieved through seeing things in their true nature as impermanent and ever-changing.

The third kind of *vipassanā* concentration, called in Pali *appanihitasamādhi*, is one which is directed toward the characteristic of unsatisfactoriness of all things (*dukkhalakkhaṇa*). The word *appanihita* means "desireless." Where this type of concentration is involved in insight meditation, the meditator directs mindfulness to the unsatisfactory aspect of experiences pertaining to the Four Foundations of Mindfulness in order to perceive things in their true nature. Such contemplation enables one to relinquish desire and attachment and leads to the realization of *Nibbāna*.

Strictly speaking, the three characteristics of existence are but different aspects of one and the same reality. As the Buddha often stressed, "Whatever is impermanent is unsatisfactory; whatever is unsatisfactory is nonself." The practitioner of insight meditation may therefore select that characteristic which is most suitable to his temperament and concentrate on that in order to make greater progress in his endeavor. For instance, a person with inherent propensity for sensual desire may practise profitably by constantly applying mindfulness to the unsatisfactory nature of things. This would serve as a direct antidote to that weakness and enable one to advance more satisfactorily on the spiritual path.

# 9

# BUDDHISM AND THAI SOCIETY

## FREEDOM OF CHOICE

LTHOUGH BUDDHISM IS THAILAND'S STATE religion, freedom to practise the religion of one's choice is guaranteed by the constitution, and all Thai citizens equally enjoy this right and prerogative. This freedom is, in fact, rooted in the spirit of tolerance, which is one of the most distinctive characteristics of the Buddha's teachings.

According to the 1990 Thai census there were 53,403,919 Buddhists in Thailand. In addition, there were 2,252,427 Moslems, 299,069 Christians, 3,606 Hindus and Sikhs, and 65,728 who profess other religions or no religion. The same census also reveals that there are 29,002 monasteries in the Kingdom, 225 of which are royal monasteries. There are 2,687 mosques, 854 Protestant churches, 331 Catholic churches, 33 Hindu and Sikh temples.

Buddhists are generally tolerant and accommodating, which is why religious persecution at Buddhist hands is unheard of in the long history of the religion. This has emboldened people of other religions to take advantage of Buddhist hospitality and tolerance by engaging in activities that are detrimental to Buddhism. We learn from history that with the Hindu overthrow of the Mauryan dynasty, around the early part of the 2nd century BC, the Hindus embarked on a massive and systematic persecution of the Buddhists, which resulted in a rapid decline of the religion in ancient India. A thousand years later they tried to wipe off whatever was left of Buddhism in the country by systematically distorting the Buddhist teachings and making Buddhism a subbranch of Hinduism. With the Moslem invasion of Sind in 710 AD, and especially when they gained more control over India in the 11th and 12th centuries, Buddhism suffered a great loss at the hands of Moslem fanatics. Buddhist monks were killed by the thousands, people were forced en masse to embrace Islam, and Buddhist monasteries were destroyed.

In contemporary Thailand, some Christian missionaries are engaged in dubious activities that are detrimental to the stability of Buddhism. They teach, for example, that the Buddha was a messenger of God, whose duty it was to prepare people in Asia for Christianity. The Buddha's enlightenment, some Christian priests claim, was God's revelation. Christian educators also make systematic efforts to reinterpret or distort the Buddha's teachings to confuse Buddhists. They have no qualms about claiming the origin of the most fundamental Buddhist doctrines, such as the Four Noble Truths, the Noble Eightfold Path, and Dependent Origination, as their own, tracing them to imaginary sources in the Bible. These and many other incidents are part of an on-going scheme to win converts to Christianity.

## FACTORS FOR THE SOLIDARITY OF BUDDHISM IN THAILAND

The appeal of the Dhamma to the Thai mentality and the ability of the religion to accommodate and transform the local culture are the most important factors underlying the Thai acceptance of Buddhism. The religion also contains within its traditions and teachings some positive characteristics that attract both ordinary laymen and intellectuals.

Since the earliest introduction of the religion, the Thais have been most liberal in their support of the Buddhist institution. Royal patronage, in particular, has always been a significant factor contributing to the stability and progress of the religion in Thailand. Following Khun Luang Mao, who was the first Thai ruler to declare himself a Buddhist, all subsequent Thai kings and rulers, without exception, were great supporters of the religion and did much to promote its advancement. Some of them, like King Lithai of Sukhothai and King Borom Trailokanath of the early Ayutthaya period, even entered the Order and trained for a time as monks. This set a precedent for a national custom: ever since then it has been a general practice for Thai men to leave home and enter the monkhood to receive monastic training for a certain period of time, at least once in their lives. Prior to his coronation as King of Thailand, King Mongkut of the Chakri dynasty in the more recent Bangkok period spent 27 years in the robes and became one of the most esteemed authorities on Buddhism and its practices. The present King and the Crown Prince also entered the monkhood for short periods.

To say that Buddhism and its practices are suitable to the Thai people is an understatement. The word 'Thai' means freedom, and this is the spirit that is most cherished by the Thai people. No other religion answers so well to that spirit as Buddhism, and this explains why the Thais feel completely at home with the religion. Also, as mentioned above, the Buddhist ecumenical outlook and philosophy seem to leave enough room for the accommodation and subsequent transformation of indigenous beliefs and practices, so that the religion not only became readily accepted by the local inhabitants, but was able in the process to bring about harmonious development in social values and traditions in the country as a whole. Thus, the royal patronage accorded to the Buddhist institution may be viewed on one hand as an expression of the King's religious devotion and personal preference, but on the other it may also be interpreted as a solid representation of the people's will and religious faith. Whatever the King does, the common people feel inclined to follow; while the King is anxious to fulfill the wants and wishes of the common people. In this way the King's actions can be said to reflect his people's aspirations.

Buddhism has become so integrated with Thai life that the two are hardly separable. Buddhist influences can be detected in Thai life-style, mannerisms, traditions, character, arts, architecture, language, and all other aspects of the Thai culture. The fact that Thailand has become widely known today as the Land of Smiles is due in no small measure to the Buddhist influence on the Thai people. Indeed, the nation as a whole owes much to the religion and wholeheartedly acknowledges her indebtedness to the Buddha's teachings.

Traditionally, Thai kings and their subjects have supported Buddhism in many different ways. They provide the four requisites of robes, food, shelter, and medicine to monks and novices, who are generally regarded by lay Buddhists as the principal guardians of the religion, and look after their other material needs. They also contribute to the construction and maintenance of monasteries and patronize monastic educational activities. Nowadays the King, as the supreme patron of the religion, appoints the Supreme Patriarch to head the Council of Elders, which is the governing body of the Saṅgha in charge of religious affairs in the country.

## DIFFERENT INTERPRETATIONS OF THE TEACHING

Differences in doctrinal interpretation and modes of practice are a common phenomenon in every major religion, including Buddhism. It is natural that living faiths will be subject to investigation and reinterpretation, which in some cases lead to differences in opinions and views. If these find sufficient support and following, the result is often the formation of a new school of thought within that particular religion.

Buddhism is an old religion. Through the course of its long and complicated history many different schools or sects have come into existence, each offering seemingly different views and interpretations on the Buddha's teachings. New modes of training have also been introduced, each claimed to have enriched the original system and made the practices more accessible and meaningful. Some schools have continued to grow, while others were little more than passing phenomena. We may regard this as a natural manifestation of events, especially since Buddhism is very much a living religion, dynamic and open. However, never has Buddhism lost its essential character, which is common throughout all its sects and denominations. Most of the apparent differences find a point of unity on a higher level of understanding, and Buddhists have no difficulty in perceiving its real message amidst the many later ramifications and developments.

The Dhamma is one, it is often stressed, but different teachers may give more emphasis to certain aspects of the Dhamma, depending on their predisposition or training. Just as the ocean has but one taste, so does the Dhamma have but one flavor, the flavor of freedom. It is possible, however, that different seekers of truth may find it more convenient to approach the Dhamma through different ways. Thus there may be more than one way to explain certain doctrinal points. At times the various approaches may give rise to confusion and uncertainty, but this state of affairs will come to an end when the Dhamma is realized on the experiential level. Just as there may be different ways to arrive at the same destination, so there may be different paths to arrive at the same truth. Once the goal has been reached, it becomes pointless to argue about methods. The best approach to solving doubt and problems is to practise and experience the Dhamma for oneself. When the

Dhamma is realized, all doubts will dissolve.

The Buddha himself might have envisaged this issue. In the discourse called *Mahāpadesa* he gave a broad criterion on which to judge if a teaching is the true Dhamma. This discourse can be used as a gauge to verify the authenticity of a teaching, and we may apply it to the instruction and practice as found in many Buddhist centres around the world. According to the *Mahāpadesa*, if a teaching is claimed to be the word of either the Buddha, the Saṅgha, a group of learned monks, or a single elder (*thera*), such teachings should neither be welcomed nor rejected without due consideration. The teaching should be compared to the doctrine and the discipline (Dhamma-Vinaya) to see if they perfectly agree with one another. "If, after thoroughly comparing them with the Discourses and the Discipline, the words and meaning fit not with the Discourses and agree not with the Discipline, then you may rightly conclude: Certainly, not from the Blessed One is the teaching, and it has been wrongly comprehended by that monk (who makes the claim). Then you should reject it. If, however ... they fit with the Discourses and agree with the Discipline, then you may rightly conclude: Certainly, from the Blessed One is the teaching, and it has been rightly comprehended." This means that we should take the Dhamma-Vinaya as the ultimate criterion for judgment of matters concerning differences in the teachings.

In a discourse given to Venerable Upāli, the Buddha similarly delineated a criterion to verify the true doctrine and discipline. According to that criterion, the true Dhamma is that which, when practised, leads to disenchantment, detachment, the extinction of *dukkha*, calm and peace, direct discernment and knowledge of the truth, enlightenment, and *Nibbāna*. Thus it can be concluded that the true Dhamma, no matter what label we give to it, is that which is conducive to the development of wisdom and understanding, and leads the practitioner to peace and happiness.

In Thailand some monastic establishments give more importance to scriptural study, some to meditation practice. Among those monasteries that function chiefly as educational centres, some are known to specialize in Abhidhamma studies, others may concentrate mainly on providing traditional ecclesiastical courses of Dhamma and Pali studies. There are also those that cater to contemporary needs with a balanced system of education that combines Dhamma studies with appropriate secular subjects to equip monks with necessary tools for future Dhamma work. Currently, there are two Buddhist universities in Bangkok, Mahachulalongkorn and Mahamakut, with their many affiliated colleges and schools throughout the Kingdom. There are also monasteries that may be considered 'unconventional,' like Buddhadāsa's Suanmokkha and Ajahn Cha's Wat Nongpapong, which strive to give training within the context of a living condition believed to closely resemble that during the Buddha's time. Even those centres that are known for their emphasis on meditation provide a wide variety of different techniques of training. Some advocate concentration as the primary objective; others emphasize insight meditation as the most important way. There are also centres that offer training in both concentration and insight meditation. If we understand the basic unity of all these establishments and know what to choose, there should be no confusion or perplexity. The vast array of choices may be viewed as an advantage, considering the different levels of spiritual maturity and development of those who are interested in Buddhist learning and practice.

## BUDDHISM AND SOCIAL PROBLEMS

Although social problems can be linked to religion, it would be naive to attribute them directly to religion. Essentially, it is the lack of true religion in the heart of people that is the root of all problems. Sometimes we take extraneous components of a religious institution, such as religious statues, buildings, and even traditional practices, rites and ceremonies, to represent religion and forget to really live the religious teachings. As a result, religion is rarely allowed to play its proper role in our personal and social lives. This leads to many problems, one of the most unfortunate of which is the fact that we hardly realize how much we lack true religion. The vicious circle seems to blind us and problems in society continue to multiply.

To be fair, problems like violence, fraud, corruption, and prostitution are not peculiar to any one particular society or nation. They are widespread social phenomena prevalent in all parts of the world, not excepting the most affluent or highly developed nations. Social problems may arise from a variety of causes and conditions for which religion can hardly be held responsible. For example, hunger and lack of suitable means for a decent livelihood may drive a basically harmless individual to an act of crime or violence. The long-term centralization of political and economic powers due to greed and megalomania may cause corruption and poverty on a large scale in the country. In fact, there are many non-Buddhist countries in the world today that are plagued with social problems of all descriptions and have not known peace for a long time. Sometimes the problems are directly related to their own religious fanaticism, which is a truly unfortunate situation.

Thai society owes a great deal to Buddhism for many of the blessings that it enjoys. There is no doubt that if more people earnestly practised the Dhamma, many of the problems Thailand now faces could be satisfactorily solved or ameliorated. For example, if people really observed the five precepts, there would be little room left for violence, fraud, and corruption. Even if only one precept of the five was adhered to, it would surely contribute tremendously to society. Indeed, it is not Buddhism that is a problem to society, but not following it in the proper way.

Buddhism is a religion of practice. This means that in order to derive benefit from the religion one needs to exert oneself and put it into practice. To call oneself a Buddhist without trying seriously to follow Buddhism will not mean much in terms of practical results. Although Thailand is a Buddhist country and the majority of the population professes Buddhism, that is hardly half the story. There still remains the need to practise the Dhamma, and if this is done by a sufficiently large number of people peace and prosperity will certainly result, and there will be less problems in society. Buddhism is a time-honored religious system; its teachings have stood the test of time for more than twenty-five centuries. The Dhamma is universally true and eternally valid. All that is needed is a sincere and earnest commitment to it.

### THE CHALLENGE OF MODERNIZATION

Through its long history Buddhism has been exposed to various cultural forces and traditions in different lands. The religion has demonstrated its excellent resilience throughout and has survived the most trying developments in human history. The scientific and logical appeal of the Buddhist teachings have consistently won new adherents and admirers in whichever lands the religion found its home. With the rapid increase of modern communications, creating an ever-shrinking world, Buddhism, which originated in the East, finds itself locked in contact with contemporary Western culture. Interestingly, new developments are taking shape.

Unlike her neighbors, which had been colonized by Western powers at one time or another, Thailand has always maintained relatively cordial relationships with the West. When the first 'farangs' (Caucasians) called at a Thai port, they were welcomed with open arms by the locals and were treated with great hospitality and friendship. Thai kings and royalty even donated large pieces of land and allowances to Christian missionaries and generously supported them in their activities. Christian churches, schools, and hospitals were built. Western culture and customs were introduced. As Thai people have always maintained a friendly attitude toward foreigners, Western influence continues to spread throughout the country, unchecked and unhindered, under the most favorable circumstances possible.

Of course, the West is at clear advantage in many respects. Modern technology impresses the Thais and the Western system of education has been adopted in lieu of the traditional one. People with a Western education have been regarded as a progressive class, while their counterparts were branded old fashioned and conservative. Gradually, more and more Thai intellectuals began to identify themselves with Western thought and values; unconsciously, they isolated themselves from traditional Thai society. In an effort to modernize the country in line with the 'more civilized' nations, Western prototypes of development were blindly followed—sometimes with devastating effects. Modernization came to be identified with Westernization and traditional Thai values came to be regarded, mostly by the so-called Western educated class, as incongruous and anachronistic in the modern Thai context.

The impact of Western influence on modern Thai society is too obvious to require any detailed examination. One may say that almost every aspect of Thai life has been touched by it—from the structure and form of government to the system of education, the economic system, commercialism and consumerism, to the arts and entertainments (where the impact is the strongest, especially among the Thai youth). Amidst these developments, Thai Buddhism is faced with a new challenge. From the perspective of religion, the impact of Christian missionary efforts in the country has been less than impressive. Despite the missionaries' best tactics and the enormous amount of money pumped into the country to support their activities, Christianity has won, until recently, only a marginal number of Thai converts. However, because Western culture is closely connected with Christianity and vice versa, what it lacks in philosophical value it amply makes up with cultural appeal and influence. This is all the more difficult for Thai Buddhists to deal with. Christianity spreads covertly in the garb of modernization and Western culture, and Thai Buddhists are caught unaware in the unremitting currents of these new developments.

For many Thais, Buddhism is closely associated with traditional values and cultural activities. But the cultural scene itself is fast changing in urban Thai society. Under the Westernized system of education, a large part of the Thai population has been alienated from Buddhism and traditional Thai culture. Gradually, Thai Buddhism finds itself more and more restricted in its role as a social and religious force. The intellectual leadership long enjoyed by the Thai Saṅgha has become much less distinct in the present, thanks in part to the misdirected process of modernization and in part to the inability of the Saṅgha to cope with the new developments sweeping through the country. Thus, the role of many Saṅgha members nowadays is more or less confined to little more than the performance of rites and ceremonies, although there are quite a few progressive monks who struggle hard to participate more meaningfully in social welfare programs and environmental issues.

So far Thailand's modernization efforts seem to have been concentrated mostly in the cities, and it is the urban populace who have shared most of the benefits from those programs. In rural areas, monks still hold social leadership among the underprivileged, with whom they maintain a comparatively close relation and cooperation. Village monasteries fulfill people's social needs and monks still fill their traditional roles of helping the villagers in their spiritual and temporal concerns. The monkhood is still greatly respected and provides a much needed opportunity for the poor to acquire a higher level of education, something not always accessible otherwise. Monks in forest meditation centers play a key role in preserving fast diminishing Thai forest reserves and wild life. They hold great potential to contribute to society. Thus, Western influence in Thailand may be drastically different in urban and rural areas, especially where Buddhism is concerned.

Fortunately, the encounter of Thai Buddhism with the West has also produced some very positive results. Many Westerners who visited the country have found in the Buddha's teachings an answer to their spiritual quest and have made Buddhism their adopted religion. Quite a few have even taken to the robes and spent the rest of their lives in monastic training. Although these cases are mainly personal spiritual pursuits, they do have an indirect influence on the Thai religious scene as a whole. These Thai trained Western monks have also played a crucial role in the growth of Buddhism in the West in recent years. Inspired by their commitment and exemplary conduct, many Thai Buddhists have begun to reexamine their religious and cultural identity. They become more serious in Buddhist studies and practice, hitherto somewhat neglected, and have grown more appreciative of Buddhist values and culture. Ironically, it is through Westerners that some Thais begin to appreciate their own spiritual heritage. Although the scope of their influence in Thailand is still limited, this development is nonetheless worth mentioning.

To say that Western influence in Thailand represents a challenge or threat to Buddhism may be an overstatement, yet its impact must be recognized. Whether the religion will continue to prosper, or how long it will survive the onslaught, will depend on how well Buddhists respond to the calls of their conscience and responsibility. As the Buddha himself stated prior to his passing away, the progress and decline of the religion lie in the hands of Buddhists. It is they who will be responsible.

# MODERN TRENDS IN THAI BUDDHISM

For Thai traditionalists Buddhism often means merit making activities such as offering food to monks or contributing to the construction projects of a monastery. Taking part in Buddhist festivals and ceremonies is also considered a meritorious act. The more devout may occasionally observe five precepts, which every lay Buddhist is expected to follow, and learn to practise basic meditation. However, they usually lack intellectual understanding of the Buddha's teachings, and take little interest in studying them, for which reason they are prone to indulge in superstition and astrology. Temple fairs and celebrations provide them with cultural entertainment and more opportunities to make merit. These people are more or less content with the status quo and expect little from their involvement with the religion other than the so-called accumulation of merits. Normally, one would not expect them to have any particular vision concerning religious or social reform, but they do contribute in no small measure to the preservation and maintenance of the Buddhist institution and the Thai culture.

Characteristically, the institution of the Thai Saṅgha is traditionalistic and conservative almost to the extreme. This conservatism represents both a weakness and a strength in the system, but in the ultimate analysis it often confines the Saṅgha to unnecessary constraint and impedes efforts by the Saṅgha to express their sense of social responsibility more fully. Even the so-called two duties of scriptural study and meditation practice, which the commentary attributes to monks and to which monks are supposed to confine themselves, have sometimes been criticized, not quite justifiably, as too restrictive and unrealistic, not reflecting the needs of the community to which the Saṅgha institution belongs. Thus, other than these two express tasks, monks are frequently seen engaged in monastic construction or renovation. Socially, their activities now rarely extend beyond the performance of religious rites and ceremonies. Public instruction or edification is often carried out perfunctorily, and the intellectual leadership which the Saṅgha previously enjoyed has weakened considerably.

Fortunately, however, there are a handful of individual Saṅgha members who are quite capable, socially conscientious, and dedicated. While not neglecting to preserve the conservative spirit of the Theravada tradition, they do make concerted efforts to relate to social needs and go out of their way to overcome the barriers and weaknesses of both traditionalism and conservatism. They run the risk of being called unconventional, but they do contribute substantially to society, in terms of both material development and spiritual well-being. Under their initiative and support, schools are built in remote rural areas, roads are constructed to connect villages, wells are dug to provide more water to villagers, funds are established to enable poor children to attend schools and colleges, family disputes are amicably settled, electricity is brought into long forgotten village settlements, etc. Some monasteries run charitable therapeutic centres for drug addicts, others establish charitable nursing homes for the aged or terminally ill AIDS patients. There are also monks who are active as environmentalists and conservation activists, who consistently try to raise public awareness in these pressing issues.

Of course, despite all these tasks, the fundamental position of scriptural study and meditative practice never suffers a setback, for there are many more monks who are traditionally active in those areas. One only hopes that there will emerge in course of time more socially engaged Saṅgha members and that the balance between conservative traditionalism and visionary farsighted pragmatism will be properly maintained.

With the phenomenal increase of Western interest in Buddhism, more Thai Buddhists have also begun to take a closer look at their own religion. One may assert that the coincidence is more accidental than incidental, but the trend is positively a welcome sign. True, this never amounts to anything close to a reform or revival movement, yet it is nonetheless quite a meaningful development. Perhaps this has been prompted, at least in part, by modern Thai political unrest and the simultaneous surge in crime and violence characteristic of moral deterioration in society. People have subsequently been forced to look for a practical alternative and solution in Buddhism, and they have found answers in the ancient message of the Buddha, which had been hitherto neglected through the headlong rush toward the material utopia. This rediscovery gives them new-found confidence in the Dhamma, which they believe may be employed to effectively stem the downhill slide of public moral consciousness. It is generally accepted that one of the causes of social problems in modern Thai society is the lack of interest in and commitment to Buddhism and Buddhist practices. This trend of spiritual disillusionment is strongest among the technocrats and the intelligentsia, hence the relatively sharp increase in their involvements with religious activities within the modern Thai social context.

With the new trend, existing meditation centres have become revitalized and new centres have been established to meet public interest. A growing number of people take to meditation. Educational establishments, such as schools, colleges, and universities, organize seminars or workshops centering on Buddhist themes for both students and the general public. Extracurricular summer courses for intensive training in Buddhist studies and monasticism are widely introduced and generously supported. More and more young men from the middle class and the intellectual sector join the Order for religious training. Although most enter the training programs for brief periods of time, the effect this has come to bear on the public moral consciousness is quite substantial. An increasing number of laity are seriously engaged in the intellectual pursuit of Buddhist scriptural knowledge, previously regarded as a strictly monastic domain, and Buddhist courses have been integrated into advanced educational curricula at university level throughout the country.

The role of lay Buddhists as Dhamma teachers in the modern religious scene should also be recognized. University courses in Buddhism, Pali, Sanskrit, and general religious studies are all taught by lay teachers, alternatively supplemented by occasional participation of invited Saṅgha members. Some lay Dhamma teachers are also active even outside their educational establishments, holding classes in Buddhism for the benefit of the general public. Even the Abhidhamma, considered more technical and therefore more difficult to comprehend, is taught and studied by interested laity. Those with a background in higher secular knowledge have the added advantage of relating it to religious understanding and are in a better position to express it, if need be, in contemporary vocabulary to make the Dhamma more intelligible and interesting.

It is worth remarking that women have also begun to take a keen interest in these intellectual pursuits, countering their previous predominant role as material supporters and their relative indifference to serious religious studies. In fact, they have now come to the forefront in the field, gaining eminence as religious instructors and forming a major part of the academic sector.

Of course, these lay academic activities are as yet rather limited, and beyond this restricted circle, monks still fill the major role of religious instructors. There are two Buddhist universities, Mahachulalongkorn and Mahamakut, both located in Bangkok, that cater to the educational needs of monks in the Kingdom, as well as those from foreign lands. These two establishments have affiliated colleges and schools in various parts of the country and offer graduate and postgraduate courses which are recognized by the Ministry of Education. They are administered solely by the respective governing bodies of monks, and the services they have rendered to the advancement of Buddhist studies have been widely recognized. Meditation is another area of specialization where the role of monks is still of the greatest significance, although some very able lay teachers are quite active in this field as well. Monk instructors do have a positive advantage, because they naturally inspire faith and respect in the practitioners and because they not only train in meditation but actually live a meditative life. Lay teachers, on the other hand, are generally more accessible and flexible, so they appeal to certain groups of people who prefer a more relaxed approach. The increased interest in recent years in the practice of meditation is, indeed, a welcome trend in contemporary Thai Buddhism.

Another important development is the recent Thai participation in international Buddhist missionary activities. Comparatively, the Thai entry into the international religious scene is long overdue, yet there are considerable resources which the country could contribute. With the West increasingly becoming interested in Buddhism, there seems to be a great demand for religious personnel to bring the Buddha's message of peace and wisdom to new and unfamiliar lands. Unfortunately, the Thai Saṅgha, especially the ecclesiastical governing body, has been slow in responding to this new opportunity. So far nothing of significance has been done in this direction, but there are individual monks who have long been active in their self-imposed foreign missions. Many have rendered quite commendable services, against all odds and, for Thai communities, the hardships of an unaccustomed environment. Thai-trained Western monks are the most successful with Western enthusiasts and the growth of their activities has been phenomenal. Presently, quite a few Thai temples, eighty-nine by the latest official figure, have been firmly established in Malaysia, Singapore, Indonesia, Australia, India, the United States, Canada, the United Kingdom, and in many parts of the European Continent. Out of these, only four are directly supported by the Thai government. However, recent attempts have been made by the Thai ecclesiastical governing body to form an institute which will deal exclusively with foreign missionary activities, and the Department of Religious Affairs is actively collaborating on the project. It is hoped that this will more effectively solve the long-standing problems with regard to the Thai role in the international Buddhist mission and will further help promote the advancement and spread of the religion in many a foreign country.

## HOW SERIOUS ARE THAIS WITH THEIR RELIGION?

It is not possible to generalize whether Thai Buddhists are serious or not about their religion. Most probably this is true of all religious institutions, within which we find varying degrees of commitment and dedication. However, unlike most other religions, which stress the importance of faith more than anything else, Buddhism places great emphasis on wisdom and understanding. Thus the level of faith and commitment to religious practice tends to depend largely on understanding and appreciation of its teachings. Naturally, this varies from one individual to another.

If generosity and friendliness were the standards by which to judge religious commitment, Thai Buddhists would no doubt be regarded as dedicated and earnest practitioners. The Thai traits of generosity and friendliness are often cited as examples of the Buddhist influence on the national personality.

Briefly speaking, there are three modes of making merit recommended by the Buddha for a lay Buddhist to follow. These are generosity (*dāna*), morality (*sīla*), and mental development (*bhāvanā*). Of these three principles, generosity is considered basic training, for it explicitly concerns outward practice. It has been pointed out that although the act of giving itself is based on an inner quality of mind, yet it is directed outwardly. The practice of morality refers to the conscious observance of moral precepts. This is said to be of higher merit and more noble than generosity, because it directly concerns the control of bodily and verbal actions. Mental development is of the highest virtue, for it deals with the training and purification of the mind, which is the most important component of the psycho-physical structure. To train the mind is to engage in the practice of meditation.

Generosity is the mode of merit making that Thai Buddhists practise more than anything else. This normally takes the form of offering food to monks, supporting the Saṅgha with material needs, contributing to monastic construction projects, or supporting charitable services. Fewer people go beyond this step to follow the moral precepts regularly. Of course, there is a customary practice of ceremonially asking for the five precepts at the beginning of every formal religious function, and most Buddhists take pains to fulfill their part in the ceremony. But, to be sure, this does not always amount to a conscious attempt to practise according to the spirit and intention of the precepts. The more devout would be an exception here. As for meditation, few are ever inclined to commit themselves to it, especially to a formal course or in a prolonged training program. Nevertheless, the recent increase of public interest in meditation may be regarded as an encouraging sign that this supreme form of merit making has finally received the attention it deserves, although one would not expect it to become a household practice.

Buddhist holy days are still considered special occasions for making merit in Thailand. There are a number of regular religious sermons or discussions on radio and television, especially on Sundays or holy days. The more important holy days, those connected with special events in the life of the Buddha, such as *Māgha*, *Visākha*, and *Āsāḷha*, are celebrated with greater enthusiasm and piety than the others. The three month period of the rains retreat is considered especially sacred for spiritual practices, and young men will leave home to enter monastic life for training as well as for merit.

One may say therefore that, on the one hand, the majority of Thai Buddhists need to commit themselves more meaningfully to the religion, yet, on the other, it may also be rightly asserted that

Buddhism in the country is still very much alive and strong. Optimistically, one hopes that things will improve, for Thailand is admittedly one of the most important strongholds of the Buddhist world today.

## BUDDHA LOCKETS AND AMULETS

It must be clear from the outset that the use of charms, talismans, and such objects as Buddha lockets or votive tablets were neither part of the Buddha's teaching, nor recommended by him. They were adopted by Buddhists in a much later period and have become popular in a comparatively recent time.

To be sure, the use of charms or talismans is a fairly widespread practice in all religions. In fact, these things are as old as civilization itself, if not older. In Buddhism, their primary introduction might have been a result of the religion's geographical proximity with Hinduism. The Tibetans are known to have practised magic and occultism since ancient times, and they might have been among the earliest Buddhists to produce such sacred objects, which were intended for protection and blessing. Spiritually advanced lamas consecrated the objects by repeatedly reciting a sacred incantation, such as *Om mani padme hum*, or by entering into a very deep state of concentration and invoking the desired power in the objects. It is believed that by so doing the energy field of the consecrated objects is transformed or intensified and the objects eventually acquire spiritually magnetic qualities with esoteric magical powers. Of course, it is further explained that the efficacy of such sacred objects depends to a large extent on the faith and confidence of the users, as well as their own favorable past *kamma*. That strong unshakable faith and conviction do produce powerful energies where the lack thereof does not is a common experience which anyone may testify from personal accounts. This is the philosophy behind the use of magic, charms, and talismans that have come into vogue through human history. Naturally, it is likely to be rejected by scientists and many intellectuals simply laugh at it.

Early Thai literature abounds with references to the use of magic and charms, testifying to the fact that such practice had been known in the country for a long time. Such practices do serve a certain purpose, but they also have severe limitations. People who lack self-confidence and a clear understanding of the doctrine of *kamma* may feel the need for some additional psychological support, which they find in such charms and magical objects. As people become more mature and have a better grasp of the Dhamma, they need less psychological support, other than that which the Dhamma provides, and are thus free from superstitious beliefs and practices.

Buddha lockets or votive tablets are only miniaturized versions of larger Buddha images. Originally, Buddha images were meant to serve as reminders of the Buddha and his virtues. Since Buddhists have the images at home for worship or meditative practice, it is natural that they would want to have them when not at home, too, such as while travelling. Thus miniature replicas of Buddha images, which could be conveniently carried around the neck, were produced by the faithful. This soon became popular and the practice was adopted by increasingly large numbers: people feel secure and auspicious when they have a Buddha image with them. Of course, since Buddha images are held in high esteem as symbolizing the Buddha and his virtues, they are duly consecrated and are treated differently from other objects. Buddhists consider them sacred and regard them with reverence.

Buddha lockets or votive tablets were also originally employed as an instrument—a skillful means, so to say—to induce people to practise the Dhamma or lead a life of righteousness. It was commonly held that whether or not one might benefit from the sacred objects depended largely on the stipulation that those who wear them must practise the Dhamma or lead a virtuous life. If people truly believed in this rationalization, they would likely be discouraged from doing wrong or evil deeds and would naturally be encouraged to do good. Although this may not strictly appear to be in keeping with the Buddhist spirit of wisdom and understanding, it does serve some practical purpose. Certainly, when the Dhamma is clearly understood one will develop a more realistic perspective and such rationalization would become irrelevant.

However, in later times the connection between Buddha lockets or votive tablets and the Dhamma seems to have been lost or forgotten altogether. Where magic is concerned, many no longer have faith in the Dhamma but have come to blindly believe in the sole powers of magic. Sacred objects cease to be an effective vehicle for the practice of Dhamma and their original, more sublime purposes are defeated. Worse still, modern day magic has become so commercialized that there are concerted efforts to spread superstition among the gullible for commercial ends. Charms and talismans are being promoted through advertising like household commodities. Surely, the need for the true Dhamma is now more urgent than ever.